GETTING THE JOB DONE!

Managing Project Teams
and Task Forces
for Success

GETTING THE JOB DONE!
Managing Project Teams
and Task Forces
for Success
Revised Edition

W. ALAN RANDOLPH
University of Baltimore

BARRY Z. POSNER
Santa Clara University

Prentice Hall, Englewood Cliffs, New Jersey 07632

Library of Congress Cataloging-in-Publication Data

RANDOLPH, W. ALAN.
     Getting the job done! : managing project teams and task forces for
success / W. Alan Randolph and Barry Z. Posner. — Rev. ed.

     p.   cm.
     Rev. ed. of: Effective project planning and management. 1987.
     Includes bibliographical references and index.
     ISBN 0-13-616285-1
     1. Industrial project management.   I. Posner, Barry Z.
     II. Randolph, W. Alan. Effective project planning and management
     III. Title.
     HD69.P75R36 1992   91-14345
     658.4'04—dc20   CIP

Editorial/production supervisor
  and interior designer: **Karen Bernhaut**
Cover designer: **Bruce Kenselaar**
Manufacturing buyers: **Kelly Behr and Susan Brunke**
Acquisitions editor: **John Willig**

© 1992 and 1988 by Prentice-Hall, Inc.
A Simon & Schuster Company
Englewood Cliffs, New Jersey 07632

Previously published as *Effective Project
Planning and Management: Getting the Job Done*

The publisher offers discounts on this book when
ordered in bulk quantities. For more information,
write:

    Special Sales/Professional Marketing
    Prentice-Hall, Inc.
    Professional & Technical Reference Division
    Englewood Cliffs, New Jersey 07632

Printed in the United States of America

10 9 8 7 6

ISBN 0-13-616285-1

Prentice-Hall International (UK) Limited, *London*
Prentice-Hall of Australia Pty. Limited, *Sydney*
Prentice-Hall Canada Inc., *Toronto*
Prentice-Hall Hispanoamericana, S.A., *Mexico*
Prentice-Hall of India Private Limited, *New Delhi*
Prentice-Hall of Japan, Inc., *Tokyo*
Simon & Schuster Asia Pte. Ltd., *Singapore*
Editora Prentice-Hall do Brasil, Ltda., *Rio de Janeiro*

To Our Wives
Ruth Anne
and
Jackie
for their Love
and Support

CONTENTS

ABOUT THE AUTHORS

W. ALAN RANDOLPH

W. Alan Randolph is department chair and professor of management at the Merrick School of Business at the University of Baltimore (Maryland). He is also a senior trainer and consultant with Blanchard Training and Development (home of *The One Minute Manager*) in San Diego, California.

Alan is an experienced consultant in areas like project management, assertive behavior, motivation, leadership, supervisory skills, management development, and organizational dynamics and has served as a trainer and consultant to both large and small companies.

He has published extensively in many professional journals. In addition, he has co-authored two books: *The Organization Game* (2nd ed., Harper-Collins, 1985) and *Managing Organizational Behavior* (Richard D. Irwin, 1989).

BARRY Z. POSNER

Barry Z. Posner is professor of management and associate dean at the Leavey School of Business and Administration, Santa Clara University (California).

Barry is an internationally recognized management educator who has planned and participated in management-development programs for numerous profit and not-for-profit organizations. He is also a recipient of the President's Distinguished Faculty Award.

In addition, Barry has published articles in a variety of professional journals and has c authored the book *The Leadership Challenge: How to Get Extraordinary Things Done in Organizations* (Jossey-Bass, 1987), which won several awards.

INTRODUCTION

The 1990s mark a time of challenge for managers throughout the world. Speed, quality, and cost have taken on increased significance in the worlds of both business and government. The new management challenge revolves around Getting the Job Done by Managing Project Teams and Task Forces for Success.

As you consider managing in this increasingly complex and dynamic world, think about the following questions:

- Do you always know what the end result of your work will look like?
- Do your supervisors, colleagues, or customers ever change their minds about what they want?
- Does your job require you to finish assignments by a specified, and short, deadline?
- Do you have more than one task to accomplish at a time?
- Do you have to get your various tasks completed with a limited set of resources?
- Do you have to work with people in other departments to get your own work done?
- Do you have to deal with conflicts about work on a regular basis?
- Do you have to somehow get people on a team to be creative and motivated?

If you answered yes to many of these questions, you have entered into the challenging world of project teams and tasks forces. Nowadays, regardless of job title, almost every manager and supervisor has responsibilities for project teams and tasks forces, at least some of the time. And all of us have felt that we could manage projects (assignments, tasks, duties, programs, promotions, campaigns, products, accounts) with greater success.

Many books have been written about management, but few of them focus on Managing Project Teams and Task Forces and the importance of Getting the Job Done. Most books talk about "shoulds," like "we should drain the swamp." But we all know how hard it is to focus on the swamp reclamation project when we are "up to our rear ends dealing with the alligators!" This book will tell you how to "train" those alligators; how to manage your projects to successful completion; how to GET THE JOB DONE!

We wrote this book to help people become better managers of project teams and task forces. Since 1980 we have been providing seminars and consulting services on Project Management, Cross Functional Teams, and Task Force Management throughout the country. We have learned a great deal from studying hundreds of projects in a variety of organizations. We have learned from the actual experiences of thousands of people who manage and work on all kinds of projects and task forces. And we have learned from the more than 15,000 people nationwide who have participated in our seminars. Through our discussions with managers and our studies of project teams and task forces, we have identified ten key rules for success. Reading this book, you will pick up proven ideas that will save you time, aggravation, and money. *Getting the Job Done!* is about *Managing Project Teams and Task Forces for Success.*

We wish you well in learning to deal effectively with this new management challenge of the 1990s.

W. Alan Randolph   *Barry Z. Posner*
Baltimore, Maryland   *Santa Clara, California*

THE CHALLENGE OF MANAGING PROJECT TEAMS AND TASK FORCES

Tomorrow's leaders will manage horizontally via projects instead of vertically via functional experts.

The time for change in the way we manage work in organizations is upon us. No longer will the traditional hierarchical organizational structure guarantee quality work getting done on time, within budget, and with zero defects. No longer will the functional approach to work promote and facilitate the kind of innovation, experimentation, and entrepreneurship that is badly needed as we approach the twenty-first century. Nothing short of a radical shift to horizontally oriented, project-focused organizations will work, according to management guru and best-selling author Tom Peters: "Routinely working across functional barriers will be seen as the way business is done. Careers will become a series of projects."

The competitive battlefront of the 1990s is time and speed to market (implementation), high quality and superior customer service, and lean and tight organization budgeting. In order to achieve a competitive advantage, indeed to even remain a player in this new race, means we must focus our energies on being innovative, while maintaining the highest quality standards, getting work done more quickly, and controlling costs. What many organizations have begun to realize is that this can only be done *across* functional lines of authority. It can only be done by people feeling empowered to use their minds and hearts, organized together in project teams and task forces.

Pioneering companies like Quad Graphics, Johnsonville Foods, Digital Equipment Corporation, Motorola, Xerox, and Procter & Gamble, to name a few, have demonstrated 30 to 40 percent increases in productivity and innovation by using cross-functional teams and by designing flatter organizational structures. They have found that organizing around project teams and task forces—that come and go with problems and opportunities—allows them to instill entrepreneurship throughout their organizations. A sense of continuous improvement through experimentation and utilization of the knowledge in the work force can best be achieved by organizing around project teams and task forces.

**More than ever successful
managers are *project* managers.**

Successfully managing projects and task forces is the bellwether skill for managers these days. Being effective working across functions and disciplines, focusing people's attentions to a common purpose, maintaining a presence even when absent, and being able to strike a balance between flexibility and planning will be among the requisite characteristics. Every successful manager will be a *project team/task force* leader—regardless of conventional title, level, or job description.[1] This book will prepare you for this challenging and essential way of **getting the job done.**

BECOMING AN EFFECTIVE PROJECT/TEAM TASK FORCE LEADER

In order to meet this new management challenge, we must begin to view ourselves as project and task force leaders, and not as

---

[1] We will use the term *project manager* generically to refer to managers in general but also to those in charge of a task force, self-directed work group, team, and the like.

traditional functional managers. From production employee to financial analyst, from banker to software developer, from engineer to administrator, we must begin to think and work with a focus on innovation and teams of people created for a specific (albeit sometimes temporary) purpose. We must begin to think of work as batched into a series of projects that have common characteristics but which are unique in focus. We must visualize innovative, project-oriented work as having the following characteristics:

1. A unique, one-time focus
2. A specific end result
3. A start and a finish
4. A time frame for completion
5. An involvement of an ad hoc, cross-functional group of people.
6. A limited set of resources
7. A sequencing of interdependent activities
8. A clear user (client, customer) of the results

Within this project team and task force world, exceptional leaders make things happen. The bottom line is that they get the job done *on time, within budget,* and *according to desired quality standards.* What is the secret to their success?

Effective project managers and task force leaders take the time necessary to plan their projects with the team and to manage that plan well. Too often, people try to complete a project without a plan. They use a "Let's fix it in the field" mentality, so it should come as no surprise when others pass them by. Effective managers of projects and task forces appreciate the need to go slow at first, so they can go fast later. Because no project ever goes 100 percent according to plan, going slow at first enables them to have a better idea about what to do when things go astray. Good planning leads to *smaller* problems during implementation, which facilitates "going faster later."

Effective project and task force leaders involve a large number of people in the planning process. They ask a lot of "What if this happens?" and "What could go wrong?" questions. They anticipate problems and disagreements and take steps to build powerful agreements out of these conflicts. They build a strong sense of commitment from people: making certain that all the groups across functions and organizational layers involved in implementing the project plan are "signed up." And they keep people informed and involved throughout implementation, soliciting their inputs and suggestions.

Effective project and task force leaders also know when to stop planning and to move into action. They have developed a sense for when the planning phase has exhausted the "What if?" questions. They understand how to find a common ground, enabling project participants to work through their inevitable disagreements.

Effective project leaders know the importance of planning; they also know when to move into action.

Effective project and task force leaders employ their power to lead the project through to implementation. They know how to develop credibility with their constituents and are able to unleash people's creative energies.

MANAGING PROJECT TEAMS AND TASK FORCES: THE RULES

The rules—and that's exactly what they are, because *no* project or task force will be successful if these rules are not followed— for project and task force success are not the providence of a divine few. We learned them as a result of our ongoing studies of people who are making a difference throughout their organizations, who are working through projects and utilizing task forces to achieve technological breakthroughs and meet competitive marketplace demands. As well, we've listened to the thousands of people who have participated in our seminars across the country and told us about their problems, concerns, and reasons why their project, task force, or team was, or was not, effective. From these efforts we have developed and over the years refined the following *ten* rules for getting the job done:

1. Set a clear **G**oal.
2. Determine the **O**bjectives.
3. Establish **C**heckpoints, **A**ctivities, **R**elationships, and **T**ime estimates.
4. Create a Picture of the **S**chedule.
5. **D**evelop people individually and as a team.
6. **R**einforce the commitment and excitement of people.
7. **I**nform everyone connected with the project.
8. **V**italize people by building agreements.
9. **E**mpower yourself and others.
10. **R**isk approaching problems creatively.

The boldfaced letters in the first four rules spell **GO-CARTS**. This is our acronym for building a good plan. Effective project managers build solid plans—**GO-CARTS**—to get them from the start of a race to the finish line.

Even the best-built **GO-CARTS**, however, will not produce a winner without a skillful **DRIVER**. And that's what the boldfaced letters in the last six rules spell. This is our acronym for what needs to happen as you implement your plan, not necessarily in any particular order but as required in the life of the project. When you know how to build effective **GO-CARTS** and develop the skills required to be a successful **DRIVER**, you can get your projects not just over the finish line but be the first to receive the coveted "checkered flag" (the symbol of victory). So, in these next ten chapters you will learn how to put into practice the rules for building your project **GO-CARTS** and for developing your skills as a project **DRIVER**—that is, how to master the rules needed to get the job done in the world of project teams and task forces.

1
Rule Number One
SET
A CLEAR GOAL

Goal setting takes lots of time and energy but you can't be successful without goals!

The first step in building the GO-CART for your project, task force, or team is to set a clear Goal. What is the desired *end* result of your project? Its scope? Amazingly, many people managing in a project environment cannot readily answer these questions! John Young, Hewlett-Packard's chief executive officer, referred to this as the challenge of "doing the right thing versus doing things right." Consider the famous example from *Alice in Wonderland* (Figure 1.1, page 8) which illustrates that "if you don't know where you're going, any road will get you there!"

In getting the job done, you must mentally start at the finish . . . and work backward. The clearer you are about the end result of your project, even though it may change, the more effectively you can plan the best way to achieve it.

Ever worked a jigsaw puzzle? You've got a thousand pieces to the puzzle—all the necessary resources to complete the project. How do you begin? By looking at the cover of the puzzle box—by studying the picture of what the pieces will look like once they are assembled properly. You start at the end result and plan backward to the beginning. Then you begin to work toward the final goal.

Since most projects require the involvement of other people, having a clear goal and being able to articulate it to others is essential. If the project team lacks a clear goal, even excellent

7

From *Alice in Wonderland*

"Cheshire Puss," she began, rather timidly, as she did not at all know whether it would like the name: however, it only grinned a little wider. "Come, it's pleased so far," thought Alice, and she went on. "Would you please tell me, please, which way I ought to go from here?"

"That depends a good deal on where you want to get to," said the Cat.

"I don't much care where" said Alice.

"Then it doesn't matter which way you go," said the Cat.

"So long as I get somewhere," Alice added as an explanation.

"Oh, you're sure to do that," said the Cat, "If you only walk long enough."

Figure 1.1   Without a Goal, You May Never Get There

skills and the best equipment will not be sufficient to ensure the team's success.

For example, suppose you gave a highly skilled archer the best equipment available and told her to start shooting, but did not tell her where the target was? The archer would shoot the arrows where she thinks is appropriate—but not necessarily at the target you had in mind (Figure 1.2). It's not that the archer isn't trying; she just does not know where to aim. She soon winds up frustrated in her efforts, and you are disappointed in the results. Time and energy are wasted. The archer has wasted her expertise and the money you spent for her fine equipment. Whose fault is this? *Yours.*

If you don't point people in the right direction, if you don't give them the big picture (for instance, showing them the picture on the jigsaw puzzle box), if you can't get them to imagine how they would feel using the product or service (the end result of your project), you are locked into an activity trap! People will be busy spinning their wheels, but nothing significant will be getting accomplished. Your team may have all the skills and equipment, but they don't know where the target is. This is called "running a well-managed bankruptcy"!

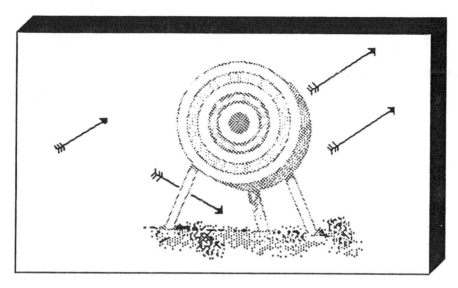

Figure 1.2 The Results of an Expert Archer Without a Clear Target

---

Without a clear goal, you may be running
a well-managed bankruptcy.

SETTING PROJECT GOALS

Many managers, as well as those in upper management, think it is easy to set goals—just state them. But it is *not* easy. It's hard work. It's also the most important action you can take at the beginning of a project or task force. What does it take to set a good project goal?

In setting a project goal, you are trying to do two things· (1) focusing yourself, your customer, and your team on the target and (2) creating commitment and agreement about the project goal. Where does this clarity of focus come from?

Project managers complain that they cannot get direction from customers and/or upper management. We have often heard people say that end users can state what they do *not* want, but not *what* they want. This is a cop-out. Goal clarification is the result of the *process* of goal setting. And it is this process that takes time, energy, and *dialogue*. It is a process of going back and forth with other people, working toward a clarity of direction for the project.

Since each project tends to be unique—it is not something that has been done before—it is difficult to be clear on a goal right away. And since goal setting is a process of dialogue, it can start in one of two ways: Top management or customers tell you what to do, or you tell top management what you see as the goal for a project. You write it down on a piece of paper and say, "Here, this is what I think the project goal is." And that gives the end user or management the option to say, "Yes, I agree. That's correct. Proceed." Or "No, that's not what I meant. Here's what I meant." And you go back and forth as you move closer and closer to achieving clarity about the direction and the end result of the project. Too many managers feel they do not have time for this goal setting process. Yet it is amazing how many have time to correct the problems that result from poor goal clarity!

The best way to capture the project goal is in a statement of project results: How will we know we are finished? What will the end result look like? Effective project managers do this by stating their goals in *user terms*. Think about this for a moment. Who is the user of your project? What does your user—client, customer, account, patient, or manager—want from you? What does the end user say you are supposed to be doing?

A user doesn't care, for example, that you are trying to produce a new accounting system (one ineffective way to describe a project's goal). The user cares about obtaining certain information about inventory and sales at the end of the day. Providing a system that meets the user's needs is your goal; designing a new accounting system is your process for doing this. Putting yourself on the user's side improves your chances of hitting the target.

In fact, if you do not define the goal in the true end user's terms, the project may be done for the wrong reasons. For example, an information system was installed at a teaching hospital for the purpose of providing patient information to the faculty for medical research purposes. Every faculty member was provided a personal computer tied to a network for access to the data. When the system was installed, no one could understand why the faculty did not use it. The administration of the hospital were the ones who wanted the system installed (because they thought it would help the faculty with their research). And since they made the contract with the consultants and paid the bills, they were perceived as the end user. But, in fact, the faculty were the true end users, and they were never consulted about the system. A great system was installed, but it did not consider the needs of the actual end users.

Setting goals requires a two-way conversation.

Effective managers of projects always try to involve the end user directly in the project, or at least to imagine the user's point of view. This is the customer perspective. Research studies point out that users originate most major technological innovations. For example, the people at Stew Leonard's phenomenally successful grocery store in Norwalk, Connecticut, have made their customers the boss. Several customers had complained that the fish wasn't fresh. This wasn't true, but the customers perceived that fish packaged in cellophane and styrofoam trays wasn't fresh. So Leonard built a fresh fish box, where fish would be purchased "fresh" off the ice. He didn't notice any fall-off in his sales of packaged fresh fish, but he started selling 100 percent more fish fresh off the ice! As Leonard explains, "Nobody comes into my store to make Stew Leonard happy. If we don't make the customers feel happy, they won't come here. And why should they? I wouldn't!"

"SMART GOALS"

In addition to establishing a goal in terms of the user, an effective project goal has five characteristics. These characteristics are captured in the term SMART, an acronym for the aspects of a goal that are likely to provide focus and create commitment. SMART goals are *s*pecific, *m*easurable, *a*greed upon, *r*ealistic, and *t*ime (cost) framed.

Specific. Your goal should be so **specific**, so well defined, so clear that anybody with some basic knowledge of the project area can read it, understand it, and know what you are trying to accomplish. You could drop dead tomorrow (of course, we do not recommend that you test it this way) and somebody else could pick up the statement of your project's goals and know exactly what to do. It should be that clearly defined.

For example, a nonspecific goal might be stated:

We need a new marketing piece.

But for what product, by whom, at what cost? To make this goal more specific, we might say:

We need a new marketing brochure for product X within three months at a cost of less than $5,000.

With this second statement, it is much clearer what needs to be accomplished. There is a far less likely chance of confusion.

Measurable.   To manage a project to successful completion, you have to be able to **measure** what the goal is. It's been said—*wrongly*—that some project goals cannot be measured. But every goal can be measured; it's just that some goals can be measured more easily than others. In fact, developing clear measuring standards for the more ambiguous and fuzzy kinds of goals is where you should spend the most time. Without measurable goals, members of your team cannot get any sense of direction, and they wind up like the archer—shooting at the wrong target. Project participants need to work on measurable activities, even if the measures are crude, in order to know what to do. And you need a measurable goal if you are to manage it.

**Every goal can be measured: it's just that some
goals can be measured more easily than others.**

For example, Ken Blanchard, co-author of *The One Minute Manager,* describes how a large bank wanted to create an image of friendliness, but nobody knew how to measure friendliness. Top management felt that bank personnel were not friendly, and a survey of customers confirmed this feeling. The consultants called in to work with the bank decided, after much discussion with bank personnel, to measure friendliness by counting the number of comments between customers and bank personnel unrelated to work—comments about the weather, about how somebody was dressed, or about how cousin Johnny was feeling these days. The consultants found that very few of the comments between bank personnel and their customers were of this nontask-related variety (about one comment per customer interaction). The goal established for the "friendliness project" was: to increase the number of nontask-related comments per customer interaction from one to four. All bank personnel got involved. They talked about the goal with the consultants, they discussed examples of what to say, and they worked at it. After five weeks of observing, the consultants determined that the number of nontask-related comments per interaction had risen to four. A follow-up customer survey revealed that their perception of the bank's friendliness had gone up dramatically. Now this is not a particularly brilliant measure of friendliness, but it worked because it helped quantify what people should do. It gave people a target they could aim at. They could also measure their own progress. Having clear measuring standards is a vital part of the process of setting good goals. Such standards as quantity, quality, time, and cost are the most useful to work with in establishing measurable standards.

Agreed upon. There must be **agreement** about the project's goals. The end user, be it a customer, upper management, or a subordinate in the organization, must agree that the project goal is desirable. Stated differently, the project manager and the project's "customer" must agree that the end result should solve the problem or respond to the need that led to the initiation of the project. The more that people agree and have clarified the goal up front, the easier it will be to develop a viable plan for the project. This agreement will make it easier to respond to changes that may require modifying the goal as the project unfolds. Agreement is based on sharing information, and it builds commitment toward the project.

Sometimes, reaching agreement can be difficult. It may take extensive dialogue to help all parties understand each other. And it usually helps if the project manager can focus on understanding what the customer/end user really needs. Those needs should be the ultimate focus for defining the agreed-upon goal.

Realistic.   Project goals must be **realistic**. All too often managers set goals that are impossible to achieve, given the resources, knowledge, and time available. Such project managers set themselves and their teams up for frustration. How many times have you been assigned a project and a deadline before the goal is clarified, only to find out that the project cannot possibly be completed on time? One of the benefits you derive from dialogue in the goal-setting process is determining whether you are talking about a goal that is realistic, given your resources. You have to question this assumption explicitly. Don't just say, "Sure, we can get that done." Discuss resources, personnel, and timing to determine how realistic the goal is. Making it realistic may mean adjusting the goal, the deadline, and/or the resources.

Realism also means that even though the project is unique and different from what you have done before, it should not be totally alien to project personnel. If it is, you are asking for trouble. In this case you will need to set aside time for research and learning, or perhaps engage consultants or hire new project members or even delay the project. You should not get trapped into doing things you know little about, unless you want to fail. This is the wisdom of "stick to your knitting," which successful companies follow. Alternatively, realize that anything worth doing well is worth doing poorly . . . in the beginning. Experience does not come freely, or even necessarily inexpensively. Build from your experiences. The goal-setting process should help you to clarify this issue.

Time (cost) framed.   Finally, you need a clear **time (cost) frame** for the goal. How much time and budget do you have to accomplish the project? Is there any flexibility in the deadline? Is there any flexibility in the resources available for the project? This goes back to looking at what is attainable. You want to set a deadline that is reasonable, given the resources available and the amount of knowledge and experience you have with this type of project.

Consider, for example, the project that God gave to Noah. God's voice boomed, "Build an ark of gopher wood, 300 cubits long, 50 cubits wide, and 30 cubits high. And do it in seven months, when I will destroy the earth by flood. Take a male and female of every animal; we are starting over."

Was that goal specific? Yes. Measurable? Not too clear on the animals but clear on the ark. Agreed upon? Who can argue with God? Noah believed in God; hence he accepted the goal. Realistic? Yes; Noah was a fisherman who knew about boats. Time (cost) framed? Yes and no. Rains were to begin in seven months; costs not clarified. But we can imagine some discussion between Noah and God about the project planning—Noah questioning God on size, type of wood, animals to be excluded, why the flood; and God explaining and refining the goal until Noah is completely clear about it. Perhaps you have similar discussions with your supervisors. The question to ask is, does your project have a SMART goal? If not, keep working at it until your project goal is SMART.

Take a few minutes to write down the goal for one of your projects. Then check it against the SMART criteria. Have you written a SMART goal: Is it specific, measurable, agreed upon, realistic, and time (cost) framed?

The importance of spending the necessary time and energy on the goal-setting process cannot be overemphasized. As one project team leader told us, "Goal setting takes lots of time and energy, but you can't be successful without goals!" Effective goal setting is crucial for your projects because it provides a common vision that gives members of the team a sense of ownership. Clear goals build excitement.

Without a SMART goal, your project is
on the path to disappointment.

Once you have a SMART project goal, you must make it a common vision for every member of the team. You need to keep everyone's eyes focused on that target until it is achieved. There are a number of things you can do to facilitate this. The first is to make certain that the goal is written down. A written goal distributed to everybody on your team will prevent people from losing sight of the goal. You should also constantly remind people that *this* is the project goal—*this* is what we are all trying to accomplish. One of the primary responsibilities of a project manager or task force leader is to keep the overall vision of the goal squarely in front of people. You need to be sure that project team members always know what they are trying to accomplish for the person or group who will ultimately use their product. Doing this improves communication, reduces tension, allows team members to evaluate how they are contributing to the goal, and ensures that your project will be completed successfully.

SUMMARY: RULE NUMBER 1 SET A CLEAR GOAL

1. Project planning begins with the end result—the goal—and works backward.
2. Effective project managers and task force leaders always keep their eyes on the goal and make sure that everybody else on the team (including the end user) is aimed in the same direction.
3. Effective project managers develop a SMART goal, ensure that it is clear, communicate it to all of their people, create a commitment to it, and make certain that team members are constantly aware of it and constantly working toward it.
4. Creating a common vision focuses every member of the project team or task force in the same direction.
5. This first step in building the vehicle which will power you to the checkered flag is extremely important. The goal is the "G" in your GO-CARTS.

Goals
O
C
A
R
T
S

2
Rule Number Two
DETERMINE
THE OBJECTIVES

People do not do what the leader expects, but what the leader inspects and rewards.

Once you have gone through the goal-setting process and have a clear idea of where the project or task force is going, you are ready to move ahead. You are ready to add more detail to your project because you cannot operate simply with a goal. Noah, for example, needed more detail than just the command "Build an ark." So does your project team. You must add the "O" to GO-CARTS and establish objectives.

Objectives are guiding principles that direct the efforts of team members in their contribution to the project's goal. Generally speaking, you need an objective for each functional group associated with the project or, in some cases, for each person involved. Team members need to know how each person will contribute to the project or task force goal. Objectives are similar to goals, but they are focused on subparts of the project.

Specifying objectives also helps you identify who needs to be on the team (i.e., what skill mix is required). Objectives breakdown the goal into a set of specific tasks. They tell each group or person what to do, when to do it, and how to measure progress. In essence, the project objectives are subgoals of the overall project goal. Accomplishment of all the objectives leads to the overall project goal. The process of defining objectives is a first step in what is often called the **Work Breakdown Structure** (see Figure 2.1, page 20).

If, for example, your project is to install a new computer

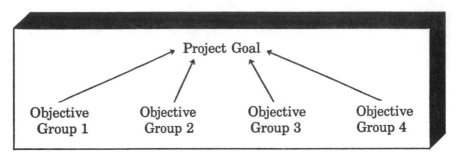

Figure 2.1   Objectives Breakdown the Goal

system, you might assign group 1 (or individual 1) the objective of preparing the site for the computer, group 2 the responsibility (the objective) of getting the computer ordered and delivered to the installation site, group 3 the responsibility of wiring the computer, and group 4 the responsibility of debugging the computer to make it operate as designed. Once these objectives are reached, your project team has completed the goal of installing a new computer system on the user's premises.

In essence, objectives resemble goals. But objectives focus on the details and tell you more about what specific people need to accomplish. They set a target for each of the various people or groups involved in a project. Just as with the goal of the project, a back-and-forth dialogue between the project leader and the groups who will complete the objectives needs to occur in order that well-defined objectives are established. You can apply the SMART criteria to each objective. An objective must be specific, measurable, agreed upon, realistic, and time (cost) framed. Otherwise, objectives cannot guide the behavior of project participants effectively.

Once you have a clear statement of project objectives, you need to identify the key project team members, resources, and inputs necessary to accomplish the overall project goal. By identifying each objective with a specific group (or a specific individual) and having a dialogue about its formulation, you establish ownership.

Ownership leads people to take responsibility and
feel committed to accomplishing the objective.

Everyone has a responsibility and must own up to that fact. Each person should understand how fulfilling that responsibility ties into the overall project goal. Many manufacturing organizations have begun to realize this process. They are redesigning their production flow so that each person feels less like a cog in the machinery and more like an essential contributor to the production process. People who help formulate their objectives tend to be more committed to accomplishing them. And objectives define the role of each team member's contribution to the overall project goal.

Just as you did for the project goal, put the project objectives in writing and literally hang them on the wall. That way they constantly remind each individual and each project group of what it is trying to accomplish. Signetics Corporation made a companywide commitment to zero defects, and everyone signed a pledge to achieve zero defects. Each of these signed statements was displayed on the lobby walls of the corporate offices. Signetics eventually *guaranteed* perfection in its shipment to all its customers.

And what about Noah and his ark? What are some of the objectives that Noah established to achieve his primary goal? Several possibilities are shown in Figure 2.2, page 22. Noah took the overall goal of building an ark and began to specify the responsibilities of the different functional groups that had to contribute to its completion.

Clarity of objectives is essential to effective project performance. Research on peak-performing individuals and groups suggests that they are always clear about their objectives. They know where they are headed. It is this sense of direction that substantially increases their chances of getting there.

PROBLEMS IN SETTING OBJECTIVES

As with goal setting, many people are not very good at setting project objectives. Objectives should be designed so that their accomplishment leads to achievement of the project goal. But as you know, there are times when it just does not work out that way. Why does this occur?

Noah's Ark Project
(Sample Objectives)

Objectives for woodcutters:

Cut 600 pieces of gopher wood, each 10 feet long by 1 foot wide by 3 inches thick. Have this done in two months.

Objectives for carpenters:

Take the 600 pieces of gopher wood and fit them together into an ark 300 cubits long, 50 cubits wide, and 30 cubits high. Do this in three months.

Objectives for the animal handlers:

Find the best-looking and strongest male and female of each species of animal. No rejects, please. Get them here in two months.

Figure 2.2 SMART Objectives for the Noah's Ark Project

Focusing Too Narrowly

Objectives alone are not enough. You must look at what tends to happen as your project personnel begin to work on their objectives. The objectives become their focus day in and day out, and it is easy for them to lose sight of the end result or project goal. It is also very easy for one group to lose sight of the objectives of the other groups working on the project or task force. People readily go off on a tangent or accomplish their objectives in a way that makes it more difficult for other team members to accomplish their objectives.

People get lost in the detail of their objectives and often lose sight of the big picture—the project goal. In other words, they fail to recognize the forest through all the trees. Manufacturing builds a product that can't be marketed on a cost-effective basis. Marketing promises customized products when operations are based on a mass production system. The key to avoiding too narrow a focus is to keep the project goal out in the open. To combat the tendency to focus too narrowly, you must constantly remind team members of the project goal.

Always keep the project goal in sight.

Reward Systems That Hurt

Reward systems in many organizations tend to push team members apart. Instead of fostering cooperation to achieve the project goal, they create competitiveness between groups as each works on its own objectives. Typically, reward systems focus on the accomplishment of the objectives for each functional group and not on the accomplishment of the project or task force goal.

A good example of this breakdown occurred at a naval air station that had four squadrons responsible for the maintenance of planes. The stated goal was to have 95 percent of all planes ready to go at any time. Actual readiness was running around 85 percent. The new commanding officer decided he would reassert this goal of 95 percent and backed it up with a reward system. Each month, he would give the *particular* squadron with the *highest* percentage of planes a reward, such as a 24-hour pass or public recognition of a job well done. What happened?

The members of one squadron decided that the secret was to have a well-stocked parts inventory. Then if a plane came in with, say, a broken radar part, they could simply take that part out and put in a replacement and the plane would be ready to go again. They also realized that if they could increase their parts inventory while decreasing the parts inventory for the other squadrons, they would be well on the way to winning this competition. The obvious solution? Steal parts! This may sound ridiculous, but it is a true story.

One of the squadrons began to engage in midnight requisitions to steal parts from the other squadrons. The other squadrons figured out what was going on and decided to retaliate. Soon four squadrons were stealing from one another. Every squadron put guards on duty 24 hours a day, seven days a week to protect its inventories. Meanwhile, the percentage of planes ready to go was going downhill fast.

The problem was the reward system. People knew the over-all goal but felt that their own squadron's objectives were more important, especially since these objectives were what was being rewarded. A simple change in the reward system solved the problem. In a given month, *any and all* squadrons that achieved the goal of 95 percent readiness would get the reward. Now, every squadron could get the reward. What happened? First, the stealing stopped. The squadrons started sharing parts to help one another out. The readiness percentage quickly rose to 90 percent and began pushing toward 95 percent—all because the reward system was changed to support the accomplishment of the objectives *and* the project goal.

As a project manager, you can't set the objectives and then forget about them. An ancient proverb captures this well: "People do *not* do what the leader *expects,* but what the leader *inspects* and *rewards.*" It is foolish to expect a result when you are not rewarding that result but are instead, rewarding some-thing else. If you want people to cooperate on a project and to keep the overall goal in mind, you will have to reward their efforts toward the project goal.

**Reward efforts that support the project *goal,*
not just the objective.**

Responsibility but Not Enough Authority

The concept of relating rewards with objectives can also help you understand why project managers often have responsi-bility but lack authority. Think about the typical setup of a project. Suppose the new company computer will affect four de-partments—data processing, accounting, production, and sales. Within each department, people report to a department manag-er. Several of these people also report to the project manager in charge of the new computer system changeover. Thus they have two bosses—their department manager and the project manag-er. The project accounts for half their responsibilities, depart-mental matters the other half. But who evaluates these people at the end of the year? The project manager? No. The department manager. So if there is any conflict in what the two managers tell the employee to do, what will the employee do? Ignore or put off the project manager. The same phenomenon affects task force participants and leaders.

For the project manager or task force approach to be successful, each person or functional group involved in the project's success must agree to cooperate and to coordinate efforts so that no employee is asked to do two things at the same time. And the project manager must have input into the evaluation of the employee (generally 50–50 with the department manager in this example, since half of the person's work is on the project). When team members know that both managers will be engaged in evaluating their performance, they are more motivated to do what *both* managers say.

But we must go one step farther and ask how we can get the data processing, accounting, production, and sales managers to cooperate with the project manager? In many cases, department managers have no real accountability for a project. But in companies where the project manager approach works best, department managers are held partly responsible for the success of the project. The division manager evaluates department managers not only in terms of department activities but also in terms of how well the project is succeeding. The department managers have a reason to cooperate and work with the project manager. Each individual department manager has a stake in the project and knows that rewards and evaluations depend on project success. The department managers focus not only on the project objectives involving their department but also on the overall success of the project. The department managers tend to cooperate and coordinate with one another and with the project manager.

Your organization may not have this kind of formalized project accountability for department managers. But if it does not, don't just throw up your hands. Instead, use the informal organization. Go outside the hierarchy to develop a relationship with each of the department managers and draw them into the project. Get them on your side and make them understand how you are going to help them. In other words, develop a relationship with the department managers.

Use the informal organization
to augment your influence.

For example, consider the situation of a marketing analyst for a large oil company. To complete projects, the analyst has to get information from salespeople in the field, but has no authority over them. To go through the organizational channels up several levels, across, and then down several levels to ask a sales rep to provide information would take months. And the sales reps have no stake in the project. So the analyst works on relationships with the salespeople. In fact, she goes out and rides the territory with the sales reps, talks with them, and gets to know them. Then, when she calls up to ask for information, it is not just the marketing analyst calling, it is their colleague. Even though the system may not support you by coordinating the objectives of different departments, you can ensure that those objectives tie in to the project goal by working through the informal organization.

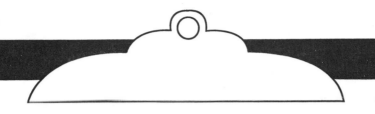

SUMMARY: RULE NUMBER 2
DETERMINE THE OBJECTIVES

1. **SMART** objectives established through dialogue break down a project or task force goal into specific tasks and commit team members to each task.
2. Objectives help identify who should be on a project team and help establish ownership by the team members.
3. Keep from focusing too narrowly on objectives and losing sight of the overall project goal.
4. Establish rewards that are linked to overall project success, as well as to success on the objectives.
5. Be certain that responsibility for a project's success carries corresponding authority.

Goals
Objectives
C
A
R
T
S

3

Rule Number Three

ESTABLISH CHECKPOINTS, ACTIVITIES, RELATIONSHIPS, AND TIME ESTIMATES

Every member of the project team needs to help plan the trip so that the best path will be taken and the road map will be clear to everyone.

GO (for Goals and Objectives) may be the propellant for your project, but you will need a **CART** to ride in. You must define, initiate, and revise as necessary checkpoints, activities, relationships, and time (cost and other resource) estimates.

It is not enough to have a goal and objectives for a project; you need checkpoints and activities to get your project completed successfully. Otherwise, how can you tell if you are going in the right direction? How will you know when to slow down or speed things up? How will you know how much time and money you will need? You must add further detail to your plan by assembling the vehicle that will take you to the finish line.

As with the project goal and objectives, there is no express lane to the checkered flag. You must roll up your sleeves and dive into a process of thinking and analyzing, as precisely as you can, what needs to be done. These steps continue the Work Breakdown Structure.

Checkpoints are like the markers that in ancient times were placed every so often along a road to let travelers know they were headed in the right direction. They served as visible reminders of progress. Checkpoints serve similar purposes in your race to the project finish line; they help you measure the progress of your project. There are both long-term and short-term checkpoints.

Checkpoint serves as visible reminders of progress.

Milestones are the long-term checkpoints. They are used to measure actual versus planned progress on projects. They are visible and tangible measures of completion. They are significant events that tell you whether your project is on schedule, behind schedule, or ahead of schedule. If, for example, you are driving from Atlanta to Los Angeles, some of the major milestones might be Birmingham, Dallas, and Phoenix. Reaching these cities would indicate that you are getting closer to your final destination. Reaching them would also indicate whether you are still on course. Missing them would mean that you had to make adjustments. For example, if you found yourself in Chicago on your trip to Los Angeles, you would know you had made a wrong turn. But clearly you would like to know this before you got so far off track. To avoid such big mistakes, you need "events."

Events are the short-term checkpoints on your route to the goal. They are similar to milestones, but they occur more frequently, and thus there are more of them. Several events usually lead up to a particular milestone. Events provide feedback on a more regular, ongoing basis. They are useful at the operational level, whereas milestones provide more of an overview. On your trip from Atlanta to Los Angeles, some of the events might be getting onto Interstate 20 heading west out of Atlanta or reaching Meridian, Mississippi, a small town between Birmingham and Dallas. Events simply add further detail to the project course. They are shorter-term then milestones. Now, if in

Atlanta you get on I-20 going east, you will know right away that you made a mistake and can correct it.

Checkpoints mark a specific instance in time, the accomplishment of something. **Activities** carry you from one event to the next, then to your milestones, and eventually to achieving project objectives and the project goal. Activities are the tasks that must be completed in order to complete the project. In defining a project, you want to identify activities as precisely and in as much detail as possible. Don't overlook any activity necessary to complete the project, no matter how small. On your trip to Los Angeles, for example, failure to check your oil at a gas station stop could halt your entire project if the car runs too low on oil.

As Figure 3.1, page 32, illustrates, goals, objectives, checkpoints, and activities are highly interrelated and are crucial in any project journey. Thinking through the checkpoints and events and beginning to list activities will typically generate additional events and milestones that you did not think of at first. Defining checkpoints and activities is a back-and-forth process. It is another step in the Work Breakdown Structure process. But remember that you begin with the larger perspective of the goal and become increasingly precise in looking at the objectives, then the milestones, the events, and the required activities. You need to go from an overall picture down to the individual details. What you are doing is working backward from the goal of the project to the first step that you have to take to get to that goal. What is the first turn you take on your trip to Los Angeles? Which way do you go out of your driveway?

THE NOAH'S ARK PROJECT

Let us take another look at Noah's project of building and stocking the ark. What were some of the milestones, events, and activities?

Consider the carpenter's objective of building the ark according to specifications. This objective involves a complex process. Milestones and events add detail to the objective; they break it down into more manageable pieces. If Noah and the carpenters had had only the objective of completing the ark, all

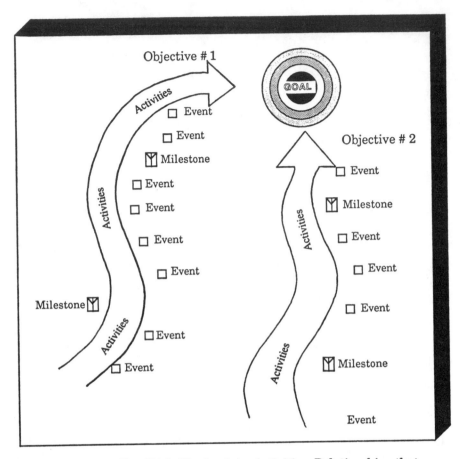

Figure 3.1 Establish Checkpoints, Activities, Relationships that Lead to the Objectives and Goal.

the thousands of additional things that were needed might never have been done, and the ark might never have been completed.

How did the milestones and events help Noah define his route and then monitor progress? Sample milestones might have been a completed layout of the ark, the skeleton of the ark built, and a male and female of each species in the waiting pen. Each milestone was a major event. By combining these with time estimates for the activities. Noah could know whether he was ahead of schedule, behind schedule, or on schedule. But had he known only that he needed to reach a milestone in a month, that might not have provided enough feedback to guide his direction and enable him to monitor his progress. He needed more specific direction.

The events provided that detail. Some of the events along the path to completing the ark's skeleton were putting the vertical supports on each side in place, nailing on the side supports, and connecting the two sides. Noah could identify several events in the process of reaching the milestone of a completed skeleton, and those events gave him more detail. Listing the events also helped him define the actions he had to complete in building the ark. When he finished determining the events and activities, he had the beginnings of a route. Adding time estimates, he could know one week into this seven-month project that he needed to have the side layout completed. He knew that if he did not have this part of the layout, he was behind schedule. If he did have the layout, he was on schedule. As he defined the first step, the second step, and the third, he made the project more manageable. This is one of the primary advantages of having checkpoints and activities. They help to define exactly what you should be doing to get a project done. An activity is more manageable than a project. Figure 3.2, page 34, summarizes part of the Work Breakdown Structure for one objective in the ark project. It focuses on the milestones, events, and activities breakdown.

MONITORING AND MOTIVATION

Milestones and events also give you a useful way to monitor progress on your project. You can continually check to determine if you are on schedule. Another valuable result that comes from having milestones, events, and activities is that they help to motivate people on the project.

Checkpoints serve as an essential form of feedback that helps project personnel stay committed and motivated. And they help team members monitor for themselves if the project is on schedule and within budget. Feedback has been called "the breakfast of champions." People thrive on it.

By giving your team members milestones and events, you set up a map for them so they can measure their location precisely. Remember the "M" in **SMART** goals and objectives.

Sample Objective for Noah's Ark Project: Carpenters Put Ark Together		
Milestones	**Events**	**Activities**
A. One Sides of ark completed	1. Side supports built 2. Sides completed 3. Railing built and mounted 4. Bottom support beam added	a. Build vertical supports b. Build horizontal supports c. Nail on slats d. Paint leak filler on slats e. Build and mount railing f. Cut ramp opening g. Nail bottom support beam
B. Second side of ark completed	(Similar to above)	

Figure 3.2 Breaking Down an Objective into Milestones, Events, and Activities

---

People need to understand the checkpoints in order to know where they are *and* where they still have to go.

Without the map, people may stray from the road and not achieve their particular objective, let alone the overall project goal.

By giving people a well-conceived set of milestones and events, you provide them with a map to track their own progress and allow them to become excited about the project. They know what the project goal is—you've reminded them of it. They know what the objective is—you've clarified that. The checkpoints and activities provide points on the map that each individual can use as a tracking system to check progress. Each person knows that the objective is to reach Dallas by Tuesday afternoon. If they pass Marshall, Texas, at noon, they know that they are on schedule. People tend to get excited when they know they are on track and making progress.

Milestones and events provide the map coordinates that help you figure out the best route to your destination (the project objectives and goal). They help you engage in contingency planning for when things get off schedule. They provide a monitoring system to help you know whether you are on or off schedule. They provide concrete feedback that makes people feel responsible and accountable. People on the project team have clear direction about where they are going, how they are being tracked, and what they need to do along the way.

Milestones and events serve to motivate team members by providing feedback and direction!

Having milestones and events also gives you an opportunity to praise progress and to recognize people's contributions. All too often, project managers overlook these opportunities. By knowing precisely what the schedule is and by being aware of it as people meet their checkpoints, you can give them a pat on the back. This does wonders in terms of energizing people and keeping them excited about the project. You don't want to be like the bowling team captain who, when a teammate knocks down seven of the ten pins on the first ball, yells, "You missed three." Effective project managers use this opportunity to say, "Fantastic. You knocked down seven. The 3, 5, and 7 pins are left. Good luck on the second ball." You are monitoring progress. You are giving feedback to people. And you are recognizing people's performance levels—praising them for their contributions and solving problems with them when they're behind schedule or not meeting expectations.

DETERMINING RELATIONSHIPS AMONG THE ACTIVITIES

Once you have a complete list of the activities that make up a project, you are ready for the next step—determining the **relationships** among the activities. Certain activities may need to

be performed before others can be performed, but some activities can be performed simultaneously. You need to lay out
the exact relationships among the activities. For example, on
the ark, Noah had to build the frame before adding the side
slats, but he could build the vertical supports at the same time
as the horizontal supports.

The questions you ask are: "What is the necessary order in
which the activities must be done?" "What is the logical flow of
activities?" and "What do technological requirements and resource availability dictate about the flow of activities?" Often
you will find that there is more than one way to do the project.
Determining the possible relationships among activities will
help you identify efficient ways to get the job done and plan for
unexpected contingencies. There is always more than one way to
get the job done, and it is important to keep this in mind.

Getting the job done seldom depends on doing things in one
right way. Perhaps two activities can be done in parallel rather
than one after the other. Perhaps an activity one group was
going to do can be done by another group. Try to anticipate the
unexpected and consider ways to deal with it.

It is at this point that you address the "What if?" and
"What could go wrong?" questions. What if this activity does not
work out the way you think it will? What are some options if you
encounter difficulties? Here you are engaged in contingency
planning, a very important element in the project-planning
process.

There are usually several ways to get to a project objective
and goal. Contingency planning helps you to focus on the alternatives in a creative fashion. You can brainstorm with the team
different ways to get a task completed; that is, different se-
quences of activities. You can also focus on what to do when
things do not go according to plan by addressing alternative
sequencing options for the activities comprising the objective
(More on contingency planning with Rule Number Four.) Just
be sure not to lose sight of your goal.

ESTIMATING TIME, COST, AND OTHER RESOURCES

In completing the Work Breakdown Structure, you also need to
determine the amount of time, money, people, equipment, and

other resources each activity will require. Such estimates allow you to plan the project more completely. Who needs to be involved in building the sides of Noah's ark? How long will it take? How much will it cost? Such decisions have to be made with limited information. Usually, you do not know exactly how long a particular activity will take. You do not know precisely what resources will be needed, or how much they will cost. This is because each project is unique. The process of estimating resource requirements is especially challenging because you cannot predict the future and because things are likely to change once you implement the plan. But with clearly defined activities it becomes possible to better identify the resources (like time and cost) needed to complete each activity.

One estimation strategy that is useful when dealing with uncertain or unfamiliar activities requires coming up with three estimates. This process works equally well for both time and cost estimates. Let us illustrate the three estimates focusing on time. The first estimate is an optimistic one—for example, the shortest possible time if everything falls into place. The second estimate is a pessimistic one—the time it will take if many things go wrong and you run into many difficulties. The third estimate is the most likely time—the time with the normal array of pluses and minuses. Such careful thinking helps you to further assess "what could go wrong" and what is really involved in completing an activity.

In making these three time estimates, it is helpful to consult with members of the team who have relevant experience about how long an activity will take. This information will help to refine your estimates. As a side benefit, involving people in the estimation process builds their commitment to the eventual time estimate, encouraging the attitude "We told Noah we could find a male and female kangaroo in two days, and, by God, we'll do it!" Recognizing that all three are still estimates, you can calculate a weighted average to get a better idea of how long the activity will take. The equation for this is shown in Figure 3.3.

The time an activity will consume will probably fall somewhere between the pessimistic and the optimistic times, and a precise estimate for the activity would be the expected time that comes out of the equation in Figure 3.3. This kind of calculation is not needed for every single activity in a project, but it is useful

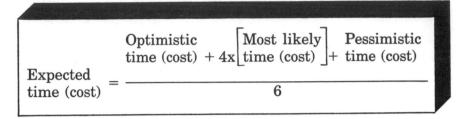

$$\text{Expected time (cost)} = \frac{\text{Optimistic time (cost)} + 4x\left[\begin{matrix}\text{Most likely}\\ \text{time (cost)}\end{matrix}\right] + \text{Pessimistic time (cost)}}{6}$$

Figure 3.3   Equation for Time (Cost) Estimates

for critical activities with which you have little experience. The same estimation process can also be used for cost considerations.

Note that in making time and cost estimates for activities, it is crucial to think through the resources needed to complete each activity. By identifying the people, equipment, and other resource needs, it becomes easier to build these cost estimates. Likewise, this resource analysis helps you to establish more realistic time estimates, as you really focus on what is involved in completing each activity.

As a general principle, however, it is always advisable to build extra resources, costs, and time (called slack) into your estimates. No one can predict the future with crystal ball certainty. Despite our best efforts at estimating, we almost always leave something out of the calculation or some unforeseen and unanticipated activity takes place. Slack is the grease effective project managers use when the project needs to be maneuvered back onto the track. But by the same token, it is not advisable to build in unnecessary slack; accurate estimates are what is desired.

The key is to spend the necessary energy to come up with as accurate an estimate of time, cost, and other resources needs, as possible, for each activity. Otherwise, your GO-CART is likely to go way off track.

**Accurate estimates are what is desired,
not estimates with lots of slack.**

Even then, it is important to recognize that these times (or costs) are *estimates*. Only after you have completed an activity will you really know how long it takes or how many other resources are needed. If you have done a similar project before, you may have a much better idea of how long it will take to complete an activity. But even then, the uniqueness of each project dictates that the resource figures you use are still estimates. Figure 3.4, page 40, shows the time estimates, the activity relationships, and who is responsible for each activity on part of the Noah's Ark project.

Sample Objective for Noah's Ark Project: Carpenters Put Ark Together

Milestones	Events	Activities	What Activities Must Precede?	Time Estimate	Who Does It?	Cost (in talents)
A. One side of ark completed	1. Side supports built	a. Build vertical supports		14 days	Noah's son Shem	250
	2. Sides completed	b. Build horizontal supports		10 days	Noah's son Ham	200
		c. Nail on slats	a, b	14 days	Shem and Ham	75
	3. Railing built and mounted	d. Paint leak filler on slats	c	7 days	Noah's son Japheth	28
	4. Bottom support beam added	e. Build and mount railing	a, b	2 days	Shem	15
		f. Cut ramp opening	d, e	1 day	Shem	5
		g. Nail bottom support beam	d	4 days	Ham and Japheth	12

Figure 3.4 The Work Breakdown Structure for One Objective in the Noah's Ark Project

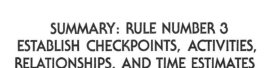

SUMMARY: RULE NUMBER 3
ESTABLISH CHECKPOINTS, ACTIVITIES, RELATIONSHIPS, AND TIME ESTIMATES

1. Develop a **CART** for your project or task force by defining **C**heckpoints to mark your progress, **A**ctivities that get the project done, **R**elationships among the activities, and **T**ime (cost and/other resource) estimates for each activity.
2. In breaking down the elements of a project, you must work backward from the goal to the very first step that you have to take to accomplish that goal.
3. People work best when they know how they are progressing toward accomplishing a goal. Establish milestones, events, and activities to help team members monitor project progress and to motivate team members.
4. Be creative and thorough as relationships among the project activities are considered. Be sure to include "What if?" and "What could go wrong?" scenarios to provide contingency planning.
5. Estimating the time and cost necessary to complete the various activities of a project is vital to an effective plan.

Goals
Objectives
Checkpoints
Activities
Relationships
Time (cost) estimates

4

Rule Number Four

CREATE
A PICTURE
OF THE SCHEDULE

A picture is worth a thousand words.

So far we have explored the essential and thorough process of planning your **GO-CART**. Unfortunately, many of us simply do not like to schedule, and that reduces both the project's and team's effectiveness. Schedules that are actually pictures of a project can make this GO-CART process more rewarding, while figuratively providing your GO-CART with a supercharger.

Studies show that successful people make the effort required to organize their time and activities. They make sure their behavior is in line with their goals. Doing the same with your projects will give you seven advantages:

1. You will have a *more realistic plan*—one that gives a more accurate picture of what will happen as your project progresses.
2. You will be better *able to anticipate* what needs to happen next.
3. You will know where to *concentrate your attention* to be sure the project stays on schedule and within the budget.
4. You will be able to *anticipate bottlenecks* and other coordination problems before they occur, so that you can take action to correct a delay *before* it becomes severe.

5. You will have a valuable tool to *enhance coordination and communication* among the project team members.

6. You will have a tool that helps to *build commitment*—because it publicly identifies responsibilities and deadlines and creates an awareness of interdependencies.

7. You will have a tool that leads to *completion* of projects *on time, within budget,* and *according to quality standards.*

To make the most of your planning efforts you have to create a picture of your GO-CART. You need to capture all of the information generated in the planning process in an easy-to-understand and easy-to-use schedule. To do this effectively, we add an "S" to the end of GO-CART to make supercharged GO-CARTS. The "S" stands for schedules. These take two basic forms: One is called a bar chart and the other a flow chart.

BAR CHARTS

Bar charts (also called Gantt charts) have proven their usefulness again and again. They are simple to draw, yet they capture a great amount of information about the project plan. They provide a useful overview of the project and constitute a quick management tool for monitoring project progress. They are equally useful with a task force effort.

A bar chart has three basic parts: a time line, a list of activities, and a bar for each activity (the length of which represents the time estimated for the activity). A statement of the goal appears at the top of the page. Figure 4.1 shows a partial bar chart for Noah's ark.

Bar charts provide an easy-to-read visual picture of activities, events, and milestones (the end points of bars mark completion of an activity). The length of the bars for each activity are proportional in length to the amount of time estimated for the activity. For example, "build vertical supports" is estimated to take 14 days and the bar is twice as long as for "paint on leak filler," estimated to take 7 days. Bar charts also show the sequencing of activities—those that must be completed before others and those that can or must be done at the same time. In the bar chart for Noah's ark, "nail on side slats" must be done prior to "paint on leak filler," but "build vertical

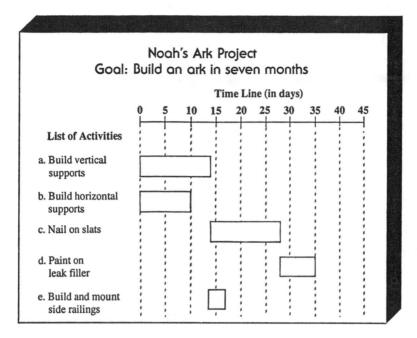

Figure 4.1 Part of a Bar Chart for Noah's Ark

supports" and "build horizontal supports" can be done at the same time (providing there are sufficient resources to do so).

The familiar saying "A picture is worth a thousand words" is certainly true in the case of a bar chart. A bar chart very quickly conveys considerable information about a project. Typically, a bar chart is drawn on one page so that you can see an entire project and the accompanying set of activities at a glance. Since you can see the entire project, you also see a picture of the project goal.

Bar charts give everyone a quick
overview of the project.

A bar chart for an entire project typically collapses many activities together and shows only major events and milestones. To provide greater detail, you create a bar chart for each objective to define tasks for the various groups and individuals on the project team or task force. For example, on the ark project,

Noah's son Shem builds the vertical supports and the side railing and cuts the opening for the ramp. A bar chart of those activities helps him know what to do and when to do it. These additional bar charts help you coordinate the efforts of various people or groups working on different objectives. In this way you can begin to see the important interface points.

You can also use the bar chart to analyze "What if?" situations and determine the best plan for a project. It is easy to move the bars around on the chart to play with different options or to make contingency plans for "What could go wrong?" situations.

Furthermore, the bar chart can be used to track and monitor progress and to provide important feedback to team members. A common way of doing this is to shade in the bars to reflect percentage of completion for an activity.

Take a look at the updated bar chart for the Ark Project (Figure 4.2). Point A on the time line reflects the current point in time. Combined with the shaded portion of the "build vertical supports" activity, you have an indication that the project is

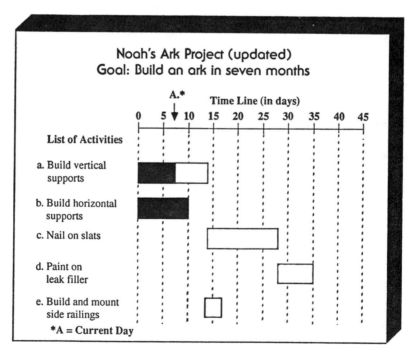

Figure 4.2   Partially Finished Project Shown on a Bar Chart

right on schedule. If the shaded portion extends to the right beyond point A, as it does for "build horizontal supports," it means you are ahead of schedule. If the shaded portion does not extend to point A, it means you are behind schedule. At a glance, you can tell where you are in relation to the schedule. If you are on or ahead of schedule, praise is called for, if you are behind, it is time for problem solving. And since a bar chart allows you to spot problems early, it makes them easier to resolve.

You can also draw a bar chart to reflect the project budget, people requirements, equipment needs, or other resource allocations. Instead of listing activities in the left margin, you could put people's names, department names, or pieces of equipment. By using the bar chart that way, your planning can avoid over-scheduling of people and equipment, especially among several projects. The bar chart can be used to track actual budget and other resource utilization versus planned utilization. Remember, you want projects done on time and according to desired quality standards, but also within budget.

Keeping your bar chart up to date as the project proceeds and examining "What if?" questions can become somewhat tedious if you must continually redraw the bar chart. Fortunately, there are many excellent computer software programs to assist with this problem. Once you have your list of activities, their relationships, and the time estimates, you can enter these data into the computer and produce a bar chart. To update the chart, you simply feed in the new information. But don't get so hooked on the computer that you forget the project! Later in this chapter we discuss choosing software appropriate for your needs.

FLOW CHARTS

Another method for drawing a picture of a project schedule is the flow chart, also called a CPM (critical path method) chart or PERT (program evaluation and review technique) chart. Flow charts were developed in the early 1950s. They are somewhat more complex to draw than bar charts. They do not provide as easy a view as bar charts of the overall project and where you currently are on the project. But flow charts are extremely useful in identifying and managing the sequential flow of critical activities in a project. Like the bar chart, the flow chart has three basic components: arrows to represent activities, small circles to represent events and milestones, and written-in time estimates. Figure 4.3 illustrates a partial flow chart for Noah's ark (events are the hollow circles, milestones the shaded ones).

The "flow" of activities is readily apparent on a flow chart (even more so than on a bar chart). It is very clear, for example, that the vertical and horizontal supports must be completed on the ark before the side slats can be nailed on, whereas vertical and horizontal supports can be built at the same time (see Figure 4.3). Also all activities, events, milestones, and time estimates are easily accessible on the flow chart. Flow charts can be used to show the sequencing of activities for projects involving literally hundreds of activities.

One advantage of a flow chart over a bar chart is that the sequencing of every activity can be clearly displayed. Also, a flow chart more clearly shows interface with other activities. This feature is extremely valuable when two interfacing activities are done by two different people. Coordination can be greatly enhanced through this picture of the project schedule.

Flow charts clearly show the sequencing of every activity.

Another advantage of a flow chart is that the longest sequence of activities in the project can easily be determined by adding up the time estimates along each path through the project. The longest path is called the "critical path" because any delays on this path will delay the entire project. The length of the critical path determines the minimum amount of time for completing the project, since all paths must be completed before the project goal is achieved. The advantage of a flow chart is that a project with hundreds of activities can be coordinated. However, a flow chart with hundreds of activities is difficult to draw, so flow charts are usually drawn in sections and separated into time blocks. Computer software is also available for creating and manipulating flow charts, thus greatly simplifying their use.

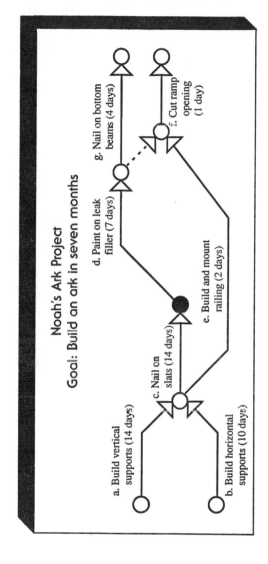

Figure 4.3 Part of a Flow Chart for Noah's Ark

WORKING WITH BAR AND FLOW CHARTS

For medium to large projects, both bar and flow charts are usually created using computer software. The flow charts aid in
daily planning and execution of work on the project. The bar
chart provides the overview that is used for coordinating and
integrating individual objectives into the overall project goals
and for monitoring budget and resource allocations. In building the ark, for example, Noah might have used a flow chart of
the entire project and given pieces of it as bar charts to the
carpenters, animal finders, food suppliers, and others. He might
also have found a bar chart useful when appraising God of the
ark's progress. It is not at all uncommon to see project managers
using both types of charts to maximize the strengths of both.
And most computer software packages provide both types of
charts as outputs from the same information input. These programs also allow you to budget and track resource use for each
activity.

Like a bar chart, a flow chart can also be used to perform
"What if?" analyses to determine the best plan for a project.
Different charts can be drawn to represent alternative ways to
complete the project. For each, the times along the paths can be
added to determine the critical path. "What if?" analysis may
enable you to figure out a way to get the project done more
quickly than was originally thought possible. Denny's restau-
rants used these techniques to reduce significantly the project
completion time on store conversion. The typical conversion cycle had been six months. But after purchasing 150 stores from
other restaurant chains, Denny's management knew they could
not take that long for each conversion. By drawing pictures (bar
and flow charts) of the conversion, and then moving boxes and
arrows around, they were able to perform "What if?" analyses
and reduce the conversion process by over 50 percent.

"What could go wrong?" analyses using a flow chart can
help you determine the impact on the project (or task force) of a
delay in any activity. You simply push the delay through the
project to determine its impact. Often, delays will have minimal
impact on overall project completion, because only delays on the
longest path cause delays in project completion. Other paths
have slack, since their total time estimates are less than that for

the longest path. It is true, however, that enough delays on the noncritical path can make that a critical path.

How a flow chart can help in managing a project can be demonstrated by examining the partial flow chart for Noah's ark in Figure 4.4, page 52. Of the seven possible paths on the flow chart, the one in bold arrows is the longest (49 days). This part of the project cannot be completed in less than 49 days. The other paths are shorter and hence have slack (extra time). For example, the path from "build horizontal supports" through "build and mount side railings" through "cut opening for ramp" is 22 days long. This means that delays of up to 27 days (49 − 22) can be tolerated on this path before the project completion date will be delayed.

Note also the dashed-line activity connecting "paint on leak filler" and "cut ramp opening." It has no name and no time attached. It is called a "dummy activity," and it is needed to show relationships in special cases. Here, for example, "Cut ramp opening" depends on both "build and mount side railings" and "paint on leak filler", but "nail on bottom support beams" depends only on "paint on leak filler." The dummy activity allows this set of relationships to be made clear.

With the flow chart in Figure 4.4 it is possible to calculate the earliest time you expect to be ready to begin, as well as the latest time you can begin each activity and still complete the project on schedule. If you add times for activities along a path moving left to right, you get the earliest start times. For example, adding the 14 days for "activity a," the 14 days for "activity c," and the 7 days for "activity d," you learn that the earliest start date for "activity f" is 35 days. The same calculation can be done via computer software for every activity in the chart, thus providing useful information for managing the project.

To calculate the latest possible start time for each activity (which still keeps the project on schedule) you work backward (right to left) in the chart subtracting activity times from the overall project time. For example, we said this project's critical path is 49 days long. By subtracting the 2 days for "activity k," then the 7 days for "activity h," and the 1 day for "activity f," we learn that the latest start date for "activity f" is 39 days. Given the 35 days earliest start date for "activity f," we find that there are 4 days of slack for this activity. For activities on the critical

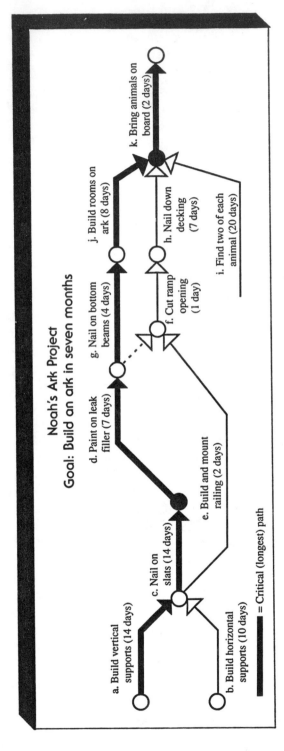

Noah's Ark Project
Goal: Build an ark in seven months

a. Build vertical supports (14 days)

b. Build horizontal supports (10 days)

c. Nail on slats (14 days)

d. Paint on leak filler (7 days)

e. Build and mount railing (2 days)

f. Cut ramp opening (1 day)

g. Nail on bottom beams (4 days)

h. Nail down decking (7 days)

i. Find two of each animal (20 days)

j. Build rooms on ark (8 days)

k. Bring animals on board (2 days)

━━━ = Critical (longest) path

Figure 4.4   A Flow Chart Example

path these calculations will reveal zero (0) days of slack for the Ark Project.

These calculations can be done for every activity in the chart, thus providing very useful information for managing the project. Certainly such calculations can be tedious and time consuming. Fortunately, there are computer software packages that help tremendously, and we will comment on these shortly.

As with the bar chart, you can update a flow chart regularly to reflect actual progress on the project. This is especially useful in determining how changes will effect the overall project completion time and for managing interfaces between various people and departments.

GETTING PROJECTS BACK ON TRACK

Flow charts and bar charts can also be quite useful in managing projects back on schedule when they fall behind. For example, slack on a particular path may indicate underutilized resources. Sometimes these resources can be shifted to the longest path to speed things along, but be careful not to shift so many resources that a noncritical path falls behind schedule and becomes a critical path. In the Noah's ark project, it is clear that there is slack on the "nail down decking" path (see Figure 4.4). Perhaps these people could help build rooms on the ark if problems are encountered.

A related way to get projects back on track is to shift slack time. Consider using the slack at the beginning, in the middle, or at the end of an activity. Noah, for example, could find the animals early in the project and hold them in a pen. Meanwhile, some of the animal finders could help on other paths of the project.

Of course, you can allocate overtime, add shifts, or bring in subcontractors to help get projects back on schedule, but you must monitor costs to keep them under control. The key here is to use your flow charts and bar charts to help you consider alternatives. By being creative and conducting "What if we did it this way?" discussions, you can use the bar charts and flow charts to analyze these alternatives and bring the project in on-time, within budget, and according to quality standards.

A NOTE ON COMPUTER SOFTWARE

As you might imagine, the planning, modification, contingency planning, and updating for complicated projects is much easier if you can use a project management software package on a computer. But it is important to recognize that a computer cannot do the steps outlined in Rules One, Two, and Three. It cannot set goals or objectives, nor can it define checkpoints, activities, relationships, and time estimates. The project team or task force must do these things before the computer can create (draw) a useful picture of the schedule. And for simple projects, resorting to the computer is probably not worth the trouble.

Computer software for projects is *only*
a tool—it cannot think for you.

Once you decide that a computer software package would be useful on your personal computer (which is what most project managers use), you embark on the project of selecting the right package from among the several hundred available on the market today. To select effectively, you first need to know what you want the software to do. For example, do you want bar chart and flow chart capabilities? What types of output reports do you want? Do you want the package to handle resource and budget allocations? Do you want it to put things on a calendar for you? How user-friendly does the software need to be? Do the software manufacturer and distributor have good reputations?

Second, you should be sure that the software package can perform at least the following functions:

1. Permits easy development and changes in project bar charts and flow charts and notes the critical path.
2. Allows you to see a bar chart or flow chart on the computer screen before printing it. And the charts are easy to follow on the screen.
3. Permits you to combine resource and budget information into the project file and to retrieve useful reports on this information.

4. Allows you to tie your project plan to a real calendar, with allowances for weekends and holidays.

5. Alerts you to overscheduling of individuals or groups, as well as to errors in the logic of your dependencies on the flow chart.

6. Allows you to construct "What if?" scenarios so that you can engage in contingency planning and update modifications.

7. Allows you to input data on project progress as the project unfolds, so you can update your plan and compare actual progress to the plan.

8. Has a good demonstration file to show you what the program can do; also has a user-friendly manual.

Third, experiment with the package on a project you have already completed. Let the package convince you that it could have helped. Above all, remember that the computer software, with its reports and files, is only a tool to help you manage the project. The computer will not manage it for you. That is your job.

SUMMARY: RULE NUMBER 4
CREATE A PICTURE OF THE SCHEDULE

1. Two common and useful methods used to plan projects and to keep them on schedule are bar charts and flow charts.
2. Bar charts provide a quick overview of a project and enable team members to easily monitor progress.
3. Flow charts are more complex than bar charts. They help to identify and manage the sequential flow of critical activities in a project.
4. By working with bar and flow charts, you can develop an effective project plan. Continuing to work with these charts *during* the project facilitates the on-time, on-budget, and on-quality completion of the project goal.

Goals
Objectives
Checkpoints
Activities
Relationships
Time (cost) estimates
Schedules

Now, just because you've built your **GO-CART(S),** your job is still not done. The plan and schedule are not the end result of the project, only the means. To get the **GO-CART(S)** to the finish line, we still need a **DRIVER.** You have to drive this vehicle to the finish line—sometimes over rough terrain, through rush-hour traffic, over forgotten bad roads and modern expressways. The skills and perspectives required to do this successfully are developed through the next six rules, making you the **DRIVER.**

5

Rule Number Five

DEVELOP PEOPLE INDIVIDUALLY AND AS A TEAM

There is a limit to what I can do by myself but no limit to what we can do together.

You have learned the importance in winning any race of having a clear picture of the finish line, of knowing the rules of the road and track conditions, of having an action plan in mind, and of being prepared for contingencies. The **GO-CARTS** process has given you the vehicle to be successful, but technique alone is insufficient without building a team of empowered people, a coalition of supporters and collaborators. You may enjoy a single victory but not a winning season. Individuals may win awards, but it is teamwork that wins championships. Are you capable of being the **GO-CARTS DRIVER?** Developing people is the first step (and the letter "D" in our second acronym).

The most basic, fundamental, and often overlooked rule about successful management—be it of projects teams or task forces—is that *You can't do it alone!* Time and again studies reveal that projects fail because the project manager has not built a strong team. This generally happens because of the project manager's insensitivity to other people. This unwillingness, or inability, to understand the perspective of others has been diagnosed as the primary reason managers are not successful in their careers.

There is no easy formula for managing people or teams. Ultimately your management strategies are based on an understanding of people and of what makes them tick, both individually and in teams. Indeed, we all know something about people. And we all have theories about why people do what they do. To be a successful project manager or team leader, you cannot be limited by your personal experience and commonsense knowledge of human and group behavior. Most important, you need to know how to put yourself in the other person's shoes. To manage the members of your project team, you must understand the fundamental nature of human behavior and appreciate other people's motivations. This information will increase your awareness of your own motivation. As Noah learned about himself and his own needs and values, he also learned how to build a strong project team. And without the team he could never have completed the ark on time—and we would all be history!

KNOW THYSELF

To understand what makes other people tick, you must first understand yourself. You learn who you are by reflecting on your experiences. Noah's commitment to God was tested and challenged, and ultimately strengthened, by God's request of him to lead the ark project. One way to understand more about yourself is to reflect on your past experiences. Where have you been victorious? What contributed to your success? How did you feel? Where have been your disappointments? What would you do differently? Can you articulate the lessons from your life, from the peaks as well as the valleys?

**To understand what makes other
people tick—first understand yourself.**

For example, when you complete a project, time and energy should be devoted to the questions "What did we learn?" How could we have accomplished this better?" and "What will we do similarly or differently next time?" Doing this leads to an accumulation of experiential learnings, rather than ten years of experience being the result of one year's experience repeated ten times. Sports teams, for example, review their performance after each game—not just at the end of the season.

Through postproject reviews you can learn what you did well so that you can incorporate these lessons into future programs. You can also note things that did not work out so that you can avoid these mistakes in the future. "Project amnesia" is likely to set in otherwise, meaning that you only remember the high points of a project and forget the low points. The postproject completion review also serves as a useful reference document each time a project is begun that is similar to a previous one.

Of course, don't assume that what motivates you will necessarily be the same for the other people on your project team. We may all be working together to develop a new software application or striving to find an antidote for AIDS, but we may likely be working for both similar (e.g., salary) and different (e.g., state-of-the-art research) reasons. And even when there are similarities, the importance attached may be different.

With enhanced self-awareness, you can begin to understand and appreciate the vast array of reasons for why people do what they do. People who are clueless about the reasons for their own behavior have little basis upon which to frame ideas about what makes others behave as they do.

Another important reason for self-awareness is that each of us has expectations about other people which create blinders that cause us to limit our appreciation of them. Often we see what we expect to see rather than what is actually occurring. Expectations are powerful—they form frames into which we fit others' behavior. If we believe that some people on the project are lazy or certain task force members are unresponsive, we will interpret their behaviors as lazy. Only behavior that is clearly contrary to our expectations will cause us to change the way we see things. And even then we are likely to be unhappy about changing (and may not) because it means we have to admit (even if only to ourselves) that we made a mistake!

Expectations also influence our attitudes and behavior toward other people. This tendency has been called a "self-fulfilling prophecy." When we behave toward others according to the way we expect them to respond (for example, closely supervising those we predict will be lazy), they often will act as we expect—

because of *our* behavior. In effect, our actions create the situation we expect, thus reinforcing our initial perception.

Develop People Individually and as a Project Team

As social psychologist Douglas McGregor observed, "Managers are prisoners of their own assumptions about human nature." His propositions about "Theory X" (where employees are viewed as lazy and irresponsible) versus "Theory Y" (where employees are viewed as responsible and hardworking) show how managers' assumptions about people determine their managerial strategies. These assumptions in turn influence the way their subordinates work. Psychologists have found that rats identified to their handlers as "maze-bright" run mazes more quickly than rats introduced to their handlers as being "dumb," students identified to their teachers as "intellectual bloomers" do better on achievement tests than students who lack such a positive introduction, and job trainees pointed out to their supervisors as having "special potential" perform better than trainees not so identified. In all cases, there is no real difference between the two groups, only a difference in expectations.

It is important to know yourself and your expectations before trying to know about someone else, especially if you hope to motivate the people on our project team. How would you answer these two questions:

1. Have you ever done anything in your life that was stupid? Yes or no?
2. Have you ever met an unmotivated person? Yes or no?

Your success in motivating others is likely to result from thinking through the implications of your responses to these two questions.

ALL BEHAVIOR MAKES SENSE!

Have you ever done anything in your life that was stupid? Most of us would have to say yes (at least once). But when we reflect on that foolish behavior, did we act that way because we wanted to be stupid or foolish? Certainly not. To understand another person's behavior, we need to see it from that person's point of view. We need to ask the question "How does this behavior *make sense to that person?*" By using this perspective, we can be analytical and descriptive about what people are doing rather than evaluative and general.

Remember that your perception of reality is not always the same as someone else's. For example, it may seem stupid to you that engineering has not released the design plans, even though they are completed and already two months past due. But it makes sense to the engineers because they believe that their appeal for additional staff will be stronger if it appears that they need more personnel (that is, it takes so long to complete design plans). Or consider how it makes perfect sense and seems only fair to me when I leave the office a few hours early on Friday. After all, I'll be back in again on Saturday, and the company "owes" me some time off with my family. But to my other task force or project members, this behavior appears wrong because my departure suggests a lack of real commitment to the project. Just imagine God saying to Noah, "Noah, what are you doing getting the animals together before the ark is completed? Are you crazy?" And Noah saying, "Wait a minute, what I'm trying to do is . . .". Each person needs to understand the perspectives of other team members if the team is to work together effectively.

ALL PEOPLE ARE MOTIVATED

Have you ever met an unmotivated person? Most of us agree that we have. But this is a trick question. If it's true, individual behavior would be random and capricious—and behavior is neither. As we discussed, all actions make sense to the people doing the acting. When you respond affirmatively to this question, what you are thinking about is a person who is motivated to do something other than what you want that person to be doing. All people are motivated. The question is: "Motivated to do what?" Consequently, it is from our perspective, and not theirs, that they are *not* motivated. You should think about motivation as the area of overlap between project goals and individual goals.

All people are motivated. The
question is: "Motivated to do what?"

All behavior is directed toward the satisfaction of individual needs. Find out more about the needs, desires, wants, and goals of the members of your project team, and you have some chance of motivating their behavior—assuming that you can help them satisfy their needs.

Knowing a team member's needs is crucial because needs that are already satisfied do not motivate or influence people's behavior. It is difficult, for example, to motivate state-of-the-art engineers by threatening to fire them when they can easily go out and find another job. Furthermore, people do not focus on higher-level needs when their lower-level needs are not being met. For instance, it would be hard to encourage more innovation from a marketing group whose members are worried about whether they are going to lose their jobs, be relocated, or be phased out.

PEOPLE ARE DIFFERENT

The basic dilemma in working with people in project teams and on task forces lies in this paradox: People are alike and people are different. Although this proposition is obviously true, the way it translates into behavior is often very subtle. Maintaining a balance between treating everyone the same (or managing everyone consistently) and being sensitive to individual differences is not easy. Striving to attain such harmony is at the heart of Hewlett-Packard's famous "HP Way." Hewlett-Packard managers are expected to treat individuals with respect and dignity while coordinating their activities with consistency and continuity.

We are all alike in that we share biological needs for food, shelter, air, and water. We differ, however, in our preferences for the flavor, texture, quantity, or quality of nourishment. We are alike in that we share basic psychological needs for belonging, love, acceptance, and accomplishment. But we differ in the degree to which we want to be included or want to include others

and in our ability to love and to be affectionate. We are physio-
logically alike in that we have two eyes, two ears, a nose, a
mouth, and a mind. However, we differ in appearance, physical
condition, and mental ability. Everyone has interests, goals, and
a personality, but everyone's interests, goals, and personality
are unique. You face the challenge of balancing consistency and
equity in relating to people. Dealing with the different personalities on a project team or task force requires considerable skill
and often much ingenuity.

In addition, the challenge of motivating the efforts of the
people on your project team is complicated because no one ever
behaves consistently—probably because no two situations are
ever exactly alike. An understanding of the perceptual process
helps to explain this. Simply put, we behave in terms of our
perception of reality, and that perception is determined partly
by what's outside of us and partly by what's inside of us.

The physiological aspect of perception defines the limit of
what we can actually see, hear, smell, or feel. Yet even given
these limitations, the information gathered by our senses does
not enter our minds as raw or unprocessed data. Each person's
perception or window on the world is shaped and bounded by
upbringing and family experiences, education and training, and
cultural values. We tend to interpret information in a way that
is consistent with our beliefs, values, and attitudes, which are
shaped by larger cultural and environmental experiences. Our
perception is determined by the interaction between physiological and psychological factors.

Perceptual differences can readily influence the ways in
which project personnel respond to organizational and managerial practices. Different individuals, for example, vary in terms
of the importance they attach to job-related rewards, the style of
leadership they prefer, their need for interpersonal contact and
interaction, and their tolerance and acceptance of job responsibility. Could Noah treat everyone working on the ark the same
way? If he told his associates that they were doing a good job,
one might be flattered, while another might wonder about what
was wrong with the way he had been working, and still another
might be suspicious of Noah's motives ("Does he mean it or is he
just trying to flatter me before asking me to work overtime?").

Neither Noah nor you can treat everyone identically, even
if you wanted to. Some people may need to know that their work

is being appreciated more than others. Some will want less variety in their routines, while others will seek out new challenges. Different people must be treated differently. Remember, there is nothing so unequal as the equal treatment of unequals.

There is nothing so unequal as the equal treatment of unequals.

The implications for you as a project manager are clear. Don't expect other people to view things exactly as you do, no matter how clearly things seem to you and how certain you are about the accuracy of your point of view. Expect differences since each person filters the same information through a different screen. Be prepared to spend time talking with project personnel. Ask what turns them on, find out what they want from this project (work or job), and watch for the things that get them excited. Use this knowledge to make sense of why they behave as they do.

And expect it to take time and effort to "make a *team*" of people.

THE MAKING OF A TEAM

Understanding yourself and the other people on the project or task force is a good place to start in understanding the making of a *team*. However, the group of people who work together on a project do not just automatically become a team the day the project or task force begins. It takes time and energy to convert a group of people into a team. There are several stages of evolution through which the group of individuals must pass together in becoming a team.

When a project team is first selected and brought together, during the goal and objectives setting stages of the project life, they are a set of people each with their own perspectives, motivations, and talents. All the potential may be there for these people to become a very effective team, but they are not yet a "team." During this *orientation* stage of team development, the team members wonder what the project is really about and what their role will be. They have some anxiety about how this team will work, as compared to others they have worked with. In short, there is a certain level of confusion that you must reduce if the team is to pass through this developmental stage. For example, Noah had to clarify for the group why the ark was to be built, as well as their skepticism about Noah really talking to God. By doing so, he was able to move the group beyond orientation.

Interestingly enough, the second stage of group development is perhaps the most difficult. By clarifying the goal and objectives, as well as the team member roles, the project or task force leader creates a gap between reality and the initial expectations of the team members. Not everything is as the team members thought it would be, and this leads the group into the *dissatisfaction* stage of group development. Team members may be heard to say, "This is not what I thought it would be like." Or "What have we gotten ourselves into now?" Sounds bad, right? Maybe you have been here on project teams before; indeed, some teams never recover from this stage of development. What you must remember is that this stage is necessary in order to eventually bring a sense of common fate to the group. What they may need is someone to blame (for example, the project leader!), but what they also need is for someone to provide continued direction and encouragement. There is life after this stage.

Just because people work together doesn't make them a team.

From the pits of dissatisfaction a properly managed group will begin to emerge as a team. As the reality and the expectations come more into line with each other, and as the team members develop in their ability to work together, the *resolution* stage of development is entered. You can even feel it as the team begins to develop a sense of cohesion. It is delicate, though, and teams often want to avoid conflict during the resolution stage. You need to continue to provide encouragement, but the encouragement needs to push the group to take risks and to work through, rather than avoid, disagreements. Noah might say to his team, "Do we really want to put the lions with the sheep?"

thus helping the team deal with a potential problem. The team, without this helpful nudge, might not address this potential problem—only to have it explode on them once the ark is loaded with animals.

Ultimately, a well-managed group of people can become a high-performing team and move into the stage of *productivity*. In this stage, the team provides its own direction and encouragement, deals constructively with conflicts, and acts responsibly to complete its assignments. In fact, in this stage the leader's focus is on getting the team the resources and recognition that it needs. The project can proceed toward the goal on time, within budget, and with quality, because the team can do it on their own. But it is important to remember that getting to this stage of productivity takes time, proper management of each previous stage of development, and an understanding of the overall process of team development. At this stage Noah would be focusing his energy of dealing with God (". . . and just when will the rains begin, and how quickly, and . . ."). Without distractions, the team members can get their job done more efficiently.

One final caveat. As the team or task force nears the completion of the project, there is a *termination* stage to reckon with. As the project end comes into sight, some project members may slack off in their efforts feeling that the project is almost over. Often, a nudging (gentle) will be needed and a reminder about the importance of meeting the schedule. Some team members will experience sadness and remorse about the team's impending demise. These folks require encouragement and emotional understanding.

With all of the stages, the key question for you to keep in mind is, "What does the team need from the leader now to keep moving through the stages of development?" Do they need direction and guidance? Or do they need support and encouragement? How much of each of these do they need? Proper analysis and follow-through can transform a group of people into a high-performing **team.**

SUMMARY: RULE NUMBER 5
DEVELOP PEOPLE INDIVIDUALLY AND AS A TEAM

1. To manage teams successfully, you must understand human behavior—first your own, then the members of your team.
2. Miscommunication often results from a clash of perspectives. You need to learn how other people perceive their goals and actions and determine a common perspective for the team.
3. Every team member is likely to be motivated by something different. A critical task of the team leader is to recognize and reward the correct motivators for each team member.
4. Teams are not made in an instant. To reach the desired stage of high productivity, the team must go through the stages of orientation, dissatisfaction, and resolution. As the project nears completion, the stage of termination must also be managed.

```
G                    Develop People and Teams
  O                    R
    C                    I
      A                    V
        R                    E
          T                    R
            S
```

6

Rule Number Six
REINFORCE THE COMMITMENT AND EXCITEMENT OF PEOPLE

People just don't wash *rental* cars!

An essential part of developing people is **R**einforcing (the "R" in DRIVER) their commitment to and excitement about the project or task force goal. When this is done well, people are not simply motivated, they are *turned on*. You don't just have their arms and legs but you have their hearts and minds. Think about the difference between working with people who are in their jobs "for something to do" versus those who are in their jobs "to do something."

Several years ago a special project group at Data General was assigned the task of designing a new computer. The project manager used special rituals to get people excited and committed to the project. For example, every member of the project team passed through an initiation rite called signing up. By signing up for the project, a person agreed to do whatever was necessary to make the project succeed. This could mean forsaking family, friends, hobbies, and all vestiges of a nonwork life until the project was completed.

The reasons behind this signing-up ritual were simple. People who make this kind of commitment to a project no longer need to be coerced to work on it. They have volunteered. Indeed, the best predictor of project success is often whether or not the project participants have volunteered for the project.

If the people on your task force or project were *volunteers,* would you treat them differently?

Data General went to great lengths to get an unusually high degree of commitment to the computer design project; you will not always need this kind of commitment to a job. You will, however, need to make sure that your project team is behind the project, working in the same direction to achieve the project's goals, rather than in front of the project, acting as roadblocks to progress. To accomplish this, you need to do more than lay out the project goals and objectives and issue instructions about what to do. You need to make team members feel that they are participating in an exciting venture, guided by a shared vision of how their efforts will bring success.

Imagine the initial project meetings between Noah and his team. Noah says, "OK, who wants to help build the ark?"

Pause. "Well, what do you mean by an ark?" asks one person. Another says, "Noah, why do you think an ark is needed?" "Who told you it's going to rain?" "What do you want us to do?" says a third person. Building commitment requires that you make certain that people understand what the project is all about and how they can contribute to its accomplishment.

BUILDING COMMITMENT

Researchers have demonstrated how companies and managers build strong organizational cultures, maintaining high levels of commitment and loyalty. Basic to this process is being clear about the key company (project) values, building consensus around them, and making certain that people feel responsibility for the project's success.

Excellent companies and high-performing teams have

clearly articulated values about how they intend to run their businesses, programs, or projects. This clarity creates a shared belief among people that focusing and adhering to these values will bring them success. Research has shown that commitment, loyalty, and pride, as well as organizational productivity, are directly related to the clarity, consensus, and intensity of organizational values and standards. Correspondence between personal and organizational values significantly affects levels of individual commitment, willingness to work hard, attachment to customers, and levels of job satisfaction and effectiveness.

Making full use of the intelligence of project members is essential to the success of any project team or self-directed work team. Total quality control programs at such companies as Motorola, Hewlett-Packard, Honeywell, Schlumberger, Memorex, Polaroid, and Xerox stem from the recognition that employees at all levels have good ideas about how to improve productivity, and managers can benefit by using them.

General Electric and many other progressive companies are utilizing self-directed work teams more often. They are not subject to many of the traditional managerial controls. Indeed, the teams act as managers themselves. The teams are given considerable autonomy to make their own decisions, as if they are a small business themselves rather than submerged in a larger company.

The teams are given fairly broad goals but little further direction on how to achieve them. They tap the intelligence and abilities of team members to tackle numerous projects that greatly enhance their productive capabilities. The results have often been dramatic, with productivity increases of 30 to 40 percent.

The point is ownership. When you rent a car, do you get it washed? No! And the reason is that the car is not yours, you are not the owner. Taking care of the car is clearly someone else's job (like the rental company). Project teams achieve the best results when members feel ownership, when they have the chance to contribute their own ideas to the project and to share responsibility for making important decisions. These conditions give project team members the opportunity to experience their work as meaningful. Surveys show that this is a critical motivator for professionals today.

Commitment comes from ownership.

BUILDING EXCITEMENT

You must provide opportunities to "encourage the heart" of the members of your project team. Don't make the mistake of assuming that individuals get excited only about money. Although increases in salary or bonuses are certainly appreciated, their effort is not only short-term but you can't buy people's commitment. Successful project managers can be distinguished from those less effective by their greater use of creative (and nonfinancial) incentives. Verbal recognition of performance in front of one's peers and visible awards, such as certificates, plaques, and other tangible gifts, are powerful ways to get people's attention.

One senior bank officer placed a large bell in the middle of the office. Every time someone made a loan, he or she got to ring it. At Mervyn's Department Store, top executives send out note cards that have "I heard something good about you" printed at the top. They send them not just to other officers but also to clerks, buyers, trainees, and other line employees. "Sticker redemption parties" are held in one large manufacturing company. Employees receive stickers for "extra effort" and these stickers can be redeemed at month's end for food and beverages at the party. At North American Tool and Die Company, the person most responsible for helping the company achieve its goal of "no rejects" that month is given the "Super Person" award.

Such actions may border on the silly. However, they provide a healthy opportunity for people to recognize and share their success with others. More important, such celebrations encourage shared visions of what needs to be done, why it is important, and that as a result of individual and collective efforts, challenging goals can be realized—and celebrations do reinforce these motives far more effectively than monetary rewards can. You should always be on the lookout for ways to spread the psychological benefits of making people feel like winners. Winners contribute in important ways to the success of their projects, and most people on the project team can be winners, given the chance.

GETTING PEOPLE COMMITTED AND EXCITED

There are many ways to get people on your project committed and excited. Here are five of the most successful:

1. Create challenging possibilities.
2. Inspire a shared vision.
3. Increase visibility.
4. Empower people.
5. Spread the "attaboys" around.

1. *Create challenging possibilities* by giving people the big picture and by promoting the meaningfulness of their efforts. Make sure everyone on the project knows the overall project goal. "We're trying to build an ark that will save us from the flood. Don't lose sight of how each board you nail on will help keep the ark afloat." Your people need to know at the outset not only what they are trying to accomplish but for whom and why. To do otherwise is to foster the alienation and apathy of "it's just another job!" Tandem Computers goes to considerable effort to give every one of its employees an understanding of the company's business and five-year plan. Every employee attends a two-day seminar on this subject. In fact, studies show that when people understand *why* they are being asked to do something they are more likely to cooperate. Have you noticed the new signs at most zoos? Replacing the traditional sign around the animal cage that said "Please stand three feet from the cage" are ones marked "Animals spit." Notice any changes in where people stand relative to the cages? Letting people see the big picture boosts commitment and energy.

2. *Inspire a shared vision* of the project's purpose and goal. Your job is to create a vision of what's possible and then to show others how their own aspirations can be aligned with those of the project. When goals are shared by project team members, these people are more likely to be committed, loyal, productive, willing to put in long hours; and much less hassled and tense.

Evidence of this dedication is the T-shirt worn by members of Apple Computer's product development group: "Working 90 hours a week and loving it."

Noah's own faith in God's prophecy helped to convince others to build the ark. You cannot overemphasize the project's goal and its importance. Frequent conversations about the project (e.g., status updates) are essential, and keeping people posted helps to sustain their focus. Listening and dealing with their concerns emphatically reinforces the "we're in this together" level of commitment. Keep in mind that you can't light a fire with a wet match!

3. *Increase visibility* of the project team's efforts. Part of the magic behind schedules (bar charts and flow charts) is that they are public. They make visible the commitments of each member of the project. They make people accountable and provide ongoing feedback about results. They also provide information about critical interdependencies. Without creating this sense of interdependency, the people on your task force or team will feel little incentive to cooperate with one another or feel a shared sense of responsibility and fate. Visibility may just be the psychological glue that holds most religions together. Congregants are constantly demonstrating their beliefs together with their peers publicly. You need to "get religion" for your team by making project team members' efforts visible for one another. At companies like Action Instruments and ShareData, employees are expected to take an active interest in the company's management and success. An "info center" supplies workers with the detailed information usually given only to top managers at many companies. Everybody knows what everyone else is doing and is supposed to be doing. Hence everyone can help one another out; everyone can cooperate more effectively.

4. *Empower people* to be effective by using their intelligence and natural drive. Empowering others means giving them the resources and authority necessary to make things happen. Give your project team the chance to perform. Give them the data, the goals, and the freedom to operate. Successful managers know that giving away power in this fashion does not reduce their own power. On the contrary, as one hospital administrator exclaimed: "Since I've started being more participative—giving power away—I've never had so much authority."

This premise has been well tested. Effective project managers find that empowering others—sharing power and responsibility—results in more committed and more responsible project participants.

Putting power in the hands of others is like
investing money in a certificate of deposit:
It is guaranteed to pay high interest.

With these actions you also demonstrate your trust in other people's competencies. You build their self-confidence and tap into their internal self-esteem drives, which is a most powerful internal performance motivator.

5. *Spread the "attaboys" around* is another successful investment strategy. Seldom do people complain that they are thanked too much by their managers. Among the many purposes that milestones serve should be marking times for celebration. People want to be effective, they want to be noticed, and they want to be appreciated. Successful project managers understand that people just want to be winners. People don't begin each day with a desire to lose. It is part of your job to show people that they can win. A key characteristic of outstanding team leaders is the exuberance with which they celebrate accomplishments. Spreading the good word about the accomplishments of your people will increase their visibility and enhance their own power and reputation. Some of the credit will inevitably find its way back to you. Your ability to get people excited and committed will get noticed.

Reinforcing the commitment and excitement of the project team means motivating them. And motivation is tricky because you don't really motivate others. Rather, you allow people's motivation to be directed toward project goals. The unfortunate truth is that the average project member uses only 30 percent of his or her potential. By following the ideas given here, you can begin to tap in to the other 70 percent. The payoff can be quite large. People will work just as hard when you are not around as when you are. Your ark will get done on time, within budget, and with quality.

SUMMARY: RULE NUMBER 6
REINFORCE THE COMMITMENT AND EXCITEMENT OF PEOPLE

1. By building both a sense of commitment to the goal and excitement about the project, team leaders can encourage members to "own" the project.

2. Give people the big picture and make sure that your project or task force is not viewed as just "another job" but as a challenging possibility.

3. Demonstrate how people's values and interests are aligned both with one another and with the project goal. Be the spark that ignites the fire in others.

4. Sharing information and authority are required if people are to believe that you believe they can do the job. Responsibility without the necessary resources and authority has always been a recipe for fool's gold.

5. Commitment is enhanced when people's actions (and accomplishments) are visible to others. Be a cheerleader because there is no such thing as a cheer-manager.

G   **D**evelop People and Teams
  O   **R**einforce Commitment and Excitement
   C   **I**
    A   **V**
     R   **E**
      T   **R**
       S

7

Rule Number Seven

INFORM EVERYONE CONNECTED WITH THE PROJECT

No good idea ever entered the head through an open mouth.

Keeping people on your team Informed is essential to the success of any project. The "I" in your DRIVER acronym reminds us of the crucial role information plays in getting the best performance out of our **GO-CARTS** and the people on the team. Unfortunately, most of us do not communicate as effectively as we should. We do not keep people on the project team, upper management, our colleagues, our end users, and even sometimes ourselves properly informed. Communication problems are experienced more often than anyone would like to admit. Have you ever experienced the kind of communication problem depicted in Figure 7.1, page 78, where everyone views the same issue from different perspectives? Many of us do all too often. But stop for a minute and think about why this happens.

BARRIERS TO EFFECTIVE INFORMATION FLOW

If you think about it, you can probably come up with quite a list of reasons why communication problems exist. Most of these reasons fall into two categories of barriers: personal and organizational. Personal barriers include such things as emotions, pre-

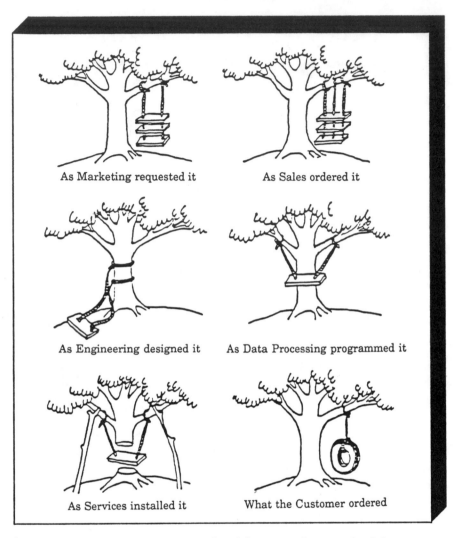

Figure 7.1 Communication breakdowns make meaningful communications difficult. (From *Let's Talk*, 2nd ed., by Sathre, Olson, and Whitney. Reprinted by permission of the authors.

occupation, hostility, past experiences, hidden agendas, inarticulateness, stereotyping, physical environment (like machine noise and telephone interruptions), daydreaming, defensiveness, and information overload.

For example, Noah's woodcutters might say, "Those carpenters wouldn't know a good board if they saw one. They're all stupid" (stereotyping). Or the thunder is crackling as they try to finish the ark. Noah says, "God, I can't hear you" (noise). Unfortunately, project team members often place greater emphasis on these personal barriers than they should. How many times have you heard "We just have a personality conflict," as though there were no hope for solution short of eliminating one or both of the team members.

Often organizational barriers are much more important in communication problems. This is because of the very nature of a task force or project team which typically involves people from different departments, who use different languages, have different objectives, have had different types of training, and yet must work together closely on a unique task. Organizational barriers to communications include an organizational structure that separates the departments, information overload or sometimes underload (too little information), ambiguity leading to incomplete information or faulty transmission of information, and time pressures.

With projects, organizational barriers to communication are often much more important than personal barriers.

For example, Noah's woodcutters cannot communicate with his animal handlers because of language differences. The trunks of animals are quite different from the trunks of trees, yet the word (trunk) is the same. Kiln-dried wood, though of critical importance to woodcutters, may not mean anything to the animal handlers. And aren't the animal selectors the most important players on the team? Just ask them.

This is an example of how the nature of your job affects your communications and problem-solving approach. Generally, manufacturing and operations personnel have short time horizons due to the fact that the outcome of their work (productivity) can be measured relatively quickly and definitively (e.g., units per hour). However, the time horizons for their counterparts in such areas as software engineering, new product development, and research are much longer. You would not measure the productivity of personnel in these functions by lines of code per hour, new products per week, or patents per month. Therefore, when you bring together these folks with the operations people on a task force, the groups have vastly different senses of urgency.

You could add several more barriers to either list, but the real issue is what you can do to overcome these barriers. What do you need to do to get your message across more effectively? What do you need to do to be a better listener?

HOW YOU CAN GET YOUR MESSAGE ACROSS

As the sender of a message, the knack is to get the other person to listen to what you are saying. Four basic practices can help you improve communications and get your message across:

1. Hit others where they are.
2. Make certain the receiver knows why your message is important.
3. Keep the other person posted.
4. Communicate assertively.

1. *Hit others where they are.* Know what is on other people's minds. What needs or problems are they thinking about? What words, phrases, examples, or analogies will make the most sense to them? Often, you know what you want to say. However, it is not as important that your message be clear to you as it is that it be clear to the person you want to receive your message. Basically, this is a marketing concept. It means that you must package your ideas in ways that make it easy for others to tune in to you. This does not mean that you have to change your idea, simply its presentation.

An example from the advertising world will make this point clear. A television commercial for a toothpaste presents two attractive people of the opposite sex. What is the advertiser trying to sell you? Toothpaste, fewer cavities, or better interpersonal relations? What the advertiser is telling you is that you too will have greater sex appeal if you use this particular brand. And the young adult market hears the message loud and clear.

But what if the intended audience is children? Do the advertisers use the same sex appeal approach: "Use your toothpaste and be the sexiest 5-year-old on the block"? Of course not. They focus in on tasting good and fighting cavities because the audience is really the parents of 5-year-olds. But the contents of the two brands are almost identical. They are just packaged and marketed differently in order to "hit others where they are." It works. Try it and you will see. But remember that it all starts with being sensitive to the needs of the person on the receiving end of your message.

**Build your message from where
others are, not where you are.**

---

2. *Make certain the receiver knows why your message is important.* People perceive the world around them in their own terms. Their terms and your terms may not be the same. Therefore, you need to understand the interests and needs of the person with whom you are communicating. The best way to get their attention is through what people in marketing refer to as "benefits selling." Consider the following example.

Burt Hinson is a very successful salesperson for a large insurance company. He has made contact with a potential new client, Jim Steward. They are meeting at Jim's house tonight to discuss Jim's insurance program. After a brief casual conversation, Burt gets to the point.

"Jim, let me ask you a few questions."

"All right," says Jim.

"Jim, do you have all the money that you really need in your life.?"

"No, of course not," responds Jim.

"OK," says Burt. "Let me ask you another question. If you were to die tomorrow, would your family have enough money for the mortgage, for living expenses, for college for your lovely kids?"

Jim hesitates, and Burt quickly holds up his hand and says, "That's OK, Jim, I understand. But let me ask you just one more question, Jim. Do you love your family?"

Gulp! Now Jim has a problem he did not have a few minutes ago. He is motivated to listen to Burt as they discuss ways to match Jim's love for his family and his financial resources. Burt, of course, is in a position to "help Jim solve his problems."

Of course, this example is a little extreme, but it makes the point. You have probably had something not too different from this happen to you. Burt has told Jim "why he should listen" and has "made it clear how his message can help him"

3. *Keeping the other person posted.* You can be a better communicator if you keep information flowing on a *regular* basis. You can accomplish this both formally (e.g., project review meetings) and informally (e.g., coffee breaks). One of the biggest mistakes many project managers make is not communicating with team members in a consistent, ongoing fashion. Furthermore, they do not communicate regularly with upper management and then seem surprised when management keeps asking what is going on.

All things considered, no one really likes surprises—neither your boss nor your project team. So keep people posted regularly!

Constantly monitoring progress along the course of the project, along with regular feedback to project team members, is the key to avoiding many communication problems. Likewise, keeping your boss or bosses informed helps to minimize the likelihood of having the rug pulled out from under you in the eleventh hour. Not surprising top management means that your requests to them will tend to be of a smaller incremental nature. Small incremental requests have a higher probability of being granted than resource requests to solve big problems.

4. *Communicate assertively with understanding.* Do you communicate assertively? Or aggressively? Many people do not understand the difference. They think that communicating assertively means making sure that they get their point across and have it acted on. But that kind of communication is really aggressive.

Figure 7.2 illustrates the difference between assertive, aggressive, and submissive communications. When you are aggressive, you promote only your ideas and try to exclude the

	Your ideas	Other's ideas
Aggressive	Used	Lost
Assertive	Heard	Heard
Submissive	Lost	Used

Figure 7.2   Framework for Understanding Aggressive, Assertive, and Submissive Communications

other person's idea. If you have the bigger club, you will probably win, at least in the short run. When you are submissive, your ideas are the ones that get lost. The other person's ideas will be adopted, assuming that he or she is also not submissive. When you are assertive, you try to be sure that your ideas are heard, but you also try to listen to the other person's ideas. The result is true communication and better problem solving because both people get their ideas out on the table and attended to.

Let's look at an example. Suppose a member of your task force comes to you and loudly says: "I've got a great idea how to handle this problem we've been having. Let me tell you. We could fire the subcontractor and redo their work ourselves by working overtime." And this person goes on and on for several minutes, then stops talking and smiles at you. Was this person assertive or aggressive? Many people would say aggressive, because it was all one-way communication and the individual did not make any effort to draw out your ideas or solicit your input.

Contrast that scene with the following scenario of the same situation. The person says, "I've got an idea how we could solve the problem we've been having. Let me tell you about it, and then I would like your reactions and ideas, too. I think we might be able to fire the subcontractor and redo their work ourselves by working overtime. What do you think?" A two-way conversation follows. Most people would say this was the assertive version because *both* parties' ideas get air time.

There are four possible outcomes when two people communicate assertively: (1) your ideas get used, (2) the other person's ideas get used, (3) a compromise of ideas gets used, and (4) the really exciting possibility—a completely new set of ideas that neither of you had thought of—emerges and gets used. Two heads really are better than one.

The key to assertive communication, and the distinction in the above two scenarios, is the concept of *understanding*. Being understanding means that you actively focus on making sense of the other person's ideas. If the person is quiet and does not volunteer thoughts, you need to draw out the person's original ideas and reactions to your ideas. If the other person is submissive, your focus will need to be almost entirely on understanding and very little on assertiveness. If the person is aggressive, your focus may shift more toward assertiveness, although understanding can also help calm down the other person. Two assertive people tend to use a relatively equal blend of assertiveness and understanding. The primary point is that by blending assertiveness and understanding, you will be focusing on the message going from sender to receiver and on the feedback going from receiver to sender. This can only improve the level of communication (and problem solving) on a project or task force.

HOW YOU CAN BECOME A BETTER LISTENER

Most project managers are not very good listeners. Yet nearly half of the time we spend in managing projects and task forces is spent in receiving information. Listening is a poorly developed skill. Tests of listening comprehension show that we typically hear only about one quarter of the information that comes to us. You can become a much better listener if you discipline yourself to follow these eight suggestions:

1. *Be prepared to listen.* Hear what the other person is trying to tell you. You have to want to hear the message coming to you. You need to scan constantly for messages. Sometimes they come very directly and clearly; at other times they are almost imperceptible. Being prepared also means cutting down on the distractions (for example, phone calls during a meeting in your office).

2. *Stop talking.* Some project managers seem to think that things will get done faster by talking more and listening less. Research shows that the best project managers learn as much as possible about what is going on by listening carefully to others.

When you stop talking you begin to create the opportunity for others to communicate their ideas and concerns. Stimulating others to talk is usually more important than listening to yourself talk! Or, as they say in the most innovative companies: "No good idea ever entered the head through an open mouth."

3. *Listen with understanding.* Put yourself in the other person's position so that you can better appreciate the language and focus on the message. If the message is unclear, you may need to use your understanding/assertive approach to clarify the message. If a team member is very angry, you may need to hear and acknowledge the anger before you can get to the real message. Remember, your primary objective when listening is to understand clearly the message being sent.

4. *Hear the speaker out completely.* Be sure you have heard the other person before you begin sending messages back. This does not mean that you cannot ask questions to clarify the message or paraphrase the message to check your interpretation. But be sure you do not cut off the person talking. Have you ever had someone complete a sentence for you? More often than not, people complete it incorrectly. Isn't this annoying? And then you must erase their mistake and try again to get your idea through to them.

Your objective when listening is to
understand the message being sent.

---

5. *Listen for what is not said.* For example, you say to one of the team members, "Sharon, would you please check the files on the shelf-life studies and summarize the results in a memo by this Friday?" Sharon responds, "Sure, I'll look into it." Sound OK? You could easily assume that Sharon will get the job done by Friday. But wait a minute. What did Sharon *not* say? She did not say that she would prepare the memo and she did not say she would do it by Friday. A little more time on the issue and checking to ensure clear communication might help avoid a disappointment for both of you on Friday.

6. *Listen for how something is said.* Pay attention to the feelings or emotional level of the message. Notice eye contact, gestures, body language, tone of voice, timing, and other nonverbal signals. Over 70 percent of our interpersonal communication is nonverbal; only 30 percent of the message is in the words we use. Imagine trying to convince Noah that some part of the ark might need to be redesigned. What he says is, "I'm open to discussing it." What you "see," however, is how he remains behind his desk, sits back in his chair, crosses his arms, sticks his jaw out, and glares at you. Listening in this way suggests that Noah may not be all that "open" and may likely require a very persuasive argument!

Or imagine a team meeting where two of the members have positioned themselves out of the circle. Two other people seem to be surveying the floor and the ceiling with their eyes. Only you and one other team member seem to be discussing working late on New Year's Eve. What do you think is going to happen when it comes time to work late on December 31? The nonverbal messages suggest that you may encounter some problems.

7. *Wait out pauses.* Give the team member who has an idea the time to share it with you fully. Wait for that department manger to collect her thoughts before she responds to your request for three of her people to work a greater percentage of their time on your project. You want people's true response, so be patient. When you are silent ("stop talking"), you invite others to fill the air with the sound of their voice.

**Patience is a virtue in encouraging
others to voice their thoughts.**

---

8. *Provide feedback.* Let others know what you heard and what you are going to do with their request, order, or information. Your primary responsibility as a listener is to understand the message being sent to you. The next most important responsibility is to let the person know you got the message. Until this loop is completed, communication has not really occurred; only transmission has. The message must be sent from the sender to the receiver, and confirmation must go back to the sender from the receiver. Then you have two-way communication.

If you are having trouble with communication on one of your projects, try instituting the "say-back rule." It works like this: John, one of your team members, says something to you.

Before you can say what you want to say, you must say back to John *in your own words* what he has said to you so that he is satisfied you got his message. If he is not satisfied, he must send it again, and you must say it back again. This goes on until he is satisfied. Then you make your point, and he must say it back to you until you are satisfied.

If you are having communication problems, this simple rule will bring them to the surface. People are often appalled at how little they have been hearing and at how hard it is to get points across among team members so that everyone is satisfied with the process. The say-back rule subtly begins making you and your project team better listeners and better senders of messages. And that is the name of the game in communication. Try it out—it works.

There is no trick to keeping people informed—effective communication is the key that unlocks the passage way from your head to others and back again. The things you can do to get your message across and the things you can do to make sure you hear what others are saying are not complex, dramatic, or necessarily difficult. Anyone can do them. You don't have to wait for anyone else to do anything differently. Working hard at sending your ideas more effectively and at being a better listener will not only make you a better communicator but will also improve the communication skills of others on your project team.

SUMMARY: RULE NUMBER 7
INFORM EVERYONE CONNECTED WITH THE PROJECT

1. Communications fail on projects because of many obstacles which can be navigated. Key are the organizational blocks brought on by the very nature of a project or task force—people from different departments working on a unique interrelated task.

2. To get your message across more effectively, (a) hit others where they are, (b) tell them why your message is important to them, (c) keep others posted regularly, and (d) communicate assertively.

3. Listening is even more important than talking. Critical steps in listening include focusing on the message, listening without talking, hearing the speaker out, and noting nonverbal signals as well as verbal ones.

```
G                   Develop People and Teams
 O                    Reinforce Commitment and Excitement
  C                      Inform Everyone
   A                       V
    R                       E
     T                       R
      S
```

8

Rule Number Eight
VITALIZE PEOPLE BY BUILDING AGREEMENTS

Conflict creates energy and effectively handling differences between people energizes everyone on the team.

You cannot get your **GO-CARTS** across the finish line in a linear fashion. While you have carefully planned and mapped out your strategy before the race, once the race starts there are likely to be unforeseen events. Moreover, there may be obstacles along the route which will only become apparent when you reach them. How to deal with these changes in your plan (which may also be positive, not just negative) is likely to create disagreements between people. Coordinating and integrating the work of different people, many of whom do not report directly to you, also raises potential conflicts.

Indeed, disagreements are unavoidable in managing projects. Studies show that project managers spend nearly half their time managing differences between team members. But the existence of disagreement and conflicts in a project is not only unavoidable; it is quite desirable. Conflicts Vitalize (hence the "V" in DRIVER) people, ensuring continued interest and commitment, encouraging novel and integrative solutions, and spotlighting potential difficulties. Energy is created by conflict.

Conflicts are born out of caring. People do not fight about

issues they don't care about. And conflict is a force that potentially unleashes people's imagination. Inherently, conflict is neither good nor bad; rather, the outcomes of conflict can be good or bad, functional or harmful, positive or negative. Marriage and family counselors often find couples divorcing because there is no conflict between the partners. At their worst they take each other for granted. The same thing can happen on your project team or task force.

**Conflict is an energizing process
to be managed, not eliminated.**

SOURCES OF CONFLICT IN PROJECTS

Many of the sources of conflict derive directly from the inherent nature of projects. Conflicts occur at various points during a project and over a variety of issues. You should take note of both where and when disagreements are likely to arise in order to manage them most effectively. Project managers and task force leaders report that conflicts typically arise over the following seven points of contention:

1. *Project priorities.* Participants have different views about the proper sequence of activities and tasks. Such differences occur not only within the project team but also between the project team and other support groups.

2. *Administrative procedures.* Disagreements arise over how a project will be managed—for example, over the definition of the project manager's reporting relationships and responsibilities, operational requirements, interdepartmental work agreements, and levels of administrative support.

3. *Technical opinions.* The less routine a project, the more likely it is that there are differences of opinions about the "best way" to accomplish the task. Disagreements may arise over specifications, technical trade-offs, and techniques to achieve the required performance. For example, the director and the film editor on a movie project may have entirely different and competing viewpoints on how best to achieve a certain effect with the camera.

4. *Staffing and resource allocations.* Conflicts arise over how best to allocate people to various projects and within project assignments. One team member complains that she always gets the "grunt work" while others get the glamorous assignments. Not only do individuals disagree over which projects their functional manager should assign them to, but they also face competing demands from their project and functional managers. This leads to both interpersonal strife and personal stress.

5. *Costs and budgets.* "How much is this going to cost?" and "Why is this costing so much?" are frequent sources of disagreement throughout a project. These differences often arise because it is difficult to estimate costs in the face of uncertainty. A functional support group, for example, may see the funds allocated by the project manager as insufficient for the work requested.

6. *Schedules.* A constant source of tension is "How long is this going to take?" The difficulty arises because so often we are dealing with estimates about the future, and the future can seldom be predicted with certainty. At the other extreme, taking into account all the contingencies—all the things that could happen—would prevent the task from getting accomplished. Further, tension is often generated around the sequencing of events, as in the case of "Finish the documentation on this project before starting to program the next portion of the new accounting system."

7. *Interpersonal and personality clashes.* Conflicts arise not just over technical issues but also over "style" or "ego-centered" issues like status, power, control, self-esteem, and friendships. Such conflicts may be based on differences that emerge from departmental or organizational factors like varying work goals and time horizons.

Our studies, as well as those of other researchers, indicate that the conflict intensity for each of these sources of conflict varies over the life cycle of a project. The tension points can often be predicted, and in such cases you should be able to manage them more effectively.

MANAGING CONFLICTS OVER THE PROJECT LIFE CYCLE

During the *formative, planning phase,* most conflicts arise over schedules, costs, priorities, and staffing. One reason that these four issues create so much turmoil is that project managers have limited control over other areas that affect these issues, particularly the functional support departments. To minimize detrimental conflict, intensive planning prior to launching the project is essential. Keeping the goal clearly in mind goes a long way toward minimizing disruptive conflicts. Involving all parties affected by the project can help you anticipate potential sources of conflict but also to begin building the team spirit necessary to resolve the differences that will occur. Every new product development team at companies like Ford and Procter & Gamble involve at least one person from marketing, engineering, and manufacturing. Think about the fact that relay teams in track run the race hundreds of times in practice before they ever step up to the starting blocks.

As a project enters the *early program phase,* conflicts arise primarily over scheduling, priorities, staffing, and technical issues. It is critical that you provide feedback on how the project is progressing and celebrate and reward early accomplishments. Frequent meetings and status review sessions help to develop interpersonal relationships that may be called upon in later, more stressful stages of the project. As the project develops, so should contingency planning about key administrative and procedural issues. It is much easier, for example, for you to discuss how a problem should be resolved and to work out a procedure for handling differences before rather than after the battle lines have been drawn.

Tension points occur for different reasons over the life of a project.

Research studies also indicate that the greater the uncertainty about the "correct" way to do the job, the more you must employ problem-solving techniques that bring people face to face rather than impersonal processes like rules and regulations. Every effort should be made to integrate as early as possible (if not right at the start) the various functional groups affected by the project. At Mervyn's Department Stores, the weekly advertising supplement is put together by the various department store managers, merchandise buyers, and marketing and financial personnel.

The *main phase* of the project finds most conflicts arising over scheduling issues. Resolving these conflicts requires continual efforts to keep people posted and to monitor work in progress. Be certain that you update and revise schedule documents and distribute them to all affected parties. Technical issues should be resolved early in the process with an emphasis on preliminary technical testing by all involved. Forecasting, thinking ahead, and communicating staffing requirements and changes can make life somewhat less hectic and anxiety-prone.

As the *end of the project* approaches, you will find conflicts developing over costs and schedules. It is important to keep team members focused on these issues. If they feel a sense of ownership in the project, they will more naturally identify with the project's success and contribute to it. Focusing on the eventual accomplishment and its significance can also tap into people's sense of pride. Noah and his new crew must have spent considerable time dreaming about the exciting possibilities before them as they waited for the waters to recede.

Letting people know what life will be like after the project is over also helps keep them focused. You may find it necessary to loosen up the tension and stress which develops as you approach final schedule deadlines and deliverables. Begin by trying not to take yourself or the situation *too* seriously. One MIS manager inserted humorous sayings into the team's computer message system over the project's final month.

BUILDING AGREEMENTS

When differences arise, you can try to reach an agreement in many ways, from giving in or smoothing over the disagreement to using threats, punishments, or withholding critical resources. The problem of persuading another person or department to adopt your point of view or to go along with your requests for project support is complicated by the fact that you typically do not possess the "power of the hierarchy." In other words, you lack formal authority. You are not the other person's boss, and you have no right to command or give orders that others are expected or obligated to follow.

One method for gaining acceptance of your viewpoint is to provide a sound rationale for your position. This is the power of intellect or expertise. People generally go along with an individual who is perceived to know what he or she is talking about (in the next chapter we will discuss the way such expertise can empower a team leader). The expression of expertise consists of communicating your rationale with reasoning and logic. Within functional areas this tactic may prove useful, but project managers or task force leaders typically operate in more than one functional area. It is difficult to have expertise across many disciplines, but you should try to be conversant across functional areas. Effective project managers and task force leaders are perceived by people in each functional area as knowing something about their discipline, but more importantly, as *appreciating* their point of view.

The more significant problem with trying to rely on reason and logic in managing differences is, quite simply, that rationality does not always prevail. Logic, data, and reason do not always point to a clear solution agreeable to another party. Competing points of view cannot be resolved by logic when each is based on a sound rationale. A likely scenario involves people from different technical backgrounds (for example, computer programming and marketing or financial analysis and production) who must arrive at a common course of action. But the bases for their discussion are so divergent that satisfactory resolution on common ground is nearly impossible. In such difficult situations, four tactics can help you build agreements in which the parties participate:

1. Create a common ground.
2. Enlarge areas of agreement.
3. Gather information.
4. Focus on issues, *not* personalities.

1. *Create a common ground.* The most important step in building agreement is to form a strong foundation: What do you

and the other person already have in common? What do the two of you agree on? What are you both trying to accomplish? Ideally, the goal of the project should sum up the common ground.

What you want to keep in mind is what you have in common, not what you disagree on. Pushing people apart at the start of a dialogue seldom engenders an atmosphere of cooperation. In agreeing on a common ground, people highlight their necessary interdependencies. When my success is a function of your success and vice versa, we are both more likely to listen and work through our differences than when our successes are viewed as independent of one another. This is, of course, one of the reasons why you should work so hard at the start of a project to involve all of the affected parties in determining the project's goal and creating a schedule (and visible schedule document) that underscores the interdependencies.

Competing points of view cannot be resolved by logic alone. Find a common ground.

---

2. *Enlarge areas of agreement.* The second step is to build on these areas of agreement. This involves moving out of the "selling your idea" or "if I can only convince them!" mode of thinking. The key to the transition from debating to building is an exchange of statements. Instead of point-and-counterpoint debates, you need to make statements and encourage the other person to do the same, such as "If you would be willing to do X, than I would be willing to do Y." This can be very hard to do because our egos get deeply entrenched in our positions. That is why you need to let go of positions in the first place and find common ground on the project, which can guide the negotiation.

A certain amount of time is needed to allow each person to get his or her ideas out on the table. Too often, however, participants in a conflict continue attacking and defending and devote little time to building an agreement. The building process is facilitated when you (1) allow each person to state his or her position without interruption, (2) allow a brief period of time for questions of clarification only, and (3) ask the question: "How can each of us get what we want?" When arguing is leading nowhere, the skilled negotiator switches to statements of possible exchange. Asking "How can each of us get what we want?" transforms the argument into a discussion and the potential deadlock into a settlement.

3. *Gather information.* An important problem-solving technique in managing conflicts is the gathering of information. Working through fundamental issues—such as "Who is in conflict?" "Who can resolve the conflict?" and "Is all the information available?"—helps to create a working foundation for dialogue. If you cannot agree which parties are really involved in the conflict, some important points of view may not be represented in the negotiations. The needs of these people will not in turn be represented in the proposed solutions.

Likewise, too often you will be arguing about, say, a scheduling problem that you and the other person cannot resolve. Disagreements about "what should have happened" often fall into this category. Discussing who should be involved in the negotiation is one way of determining what types of information are needed to build an agreement. This technique forces you to consider "Who will be affected by this agreement?" Research clearly shows that people are most likely to follow through on an agreement that they have helped shape.

4. *Focus on issues, not personalities.* Finally, it is crucial to depersonalize the conflict. When you feel that you have to defend yourself from personal attack, your response typically takes one of two forms. Either you fight back, which only escalates the disagreement and makes the possibility of finding common ground negligible, or you flee. In the latter case, you don't get people to commit their energies to problem solving. While they may agree to an action, they will have no real commitment to follow through once you are out of sight. What do the mice do when the cat is away? And in a fight, the other person's energies are devoted to getting back at you and not to solving the problem.

One of the best ways to focus on issues and not personalities is to be future oriented: "What are we going to do about this?" rather than "Why can't you be more responsible?" or "Who got us into this situation?" By being future oriented, you emphasize building agreement on a future course of action rather than blaming each other for past problems. This is not to say that you don't want to explore the past for insight into the causes of problems, but emphasizing the past often leads to one person having to defend his or her actions or blame and scapegoat someone else. "What are we going to do to insure that this doesn't happen again?" is a statement of allies *against the problem* not against each another.

SUCCESSFUL NEGOTIATORS OF CONFLICT

It is clear that successful project managers and task force leaders are effective negotiators in managing differences. Much has been written about how successful negotiators behave—what they do and what they try to avoid doing as they build agreement between people with differences. Management consultant Clifford Bolster reports in his studies that technically trained managers frequently discover that they rely too heavily on reasoning and logic in trying to get others to do what they want. He observes, "Negotiation is a process that may be used when logical reasoning has run its course and represents a critical skill for the technical manager today."

The objective of negotiation is to reach an agreement that satisfies both parties. Satisfaction is an *emotional,* not a logical, experience. Negotiation is not an optimal, dispassionate problem-solving experience where analysis and reasoning are the only skills needed to determine the cause of the problem and to reach the solution with the highest probability of solving the problem. Could Noah have *proved* that it would rain for 40 days and 40 nights or whether such a storm really would have flooded the earth?

The best solution in negotiations is the one that satisfies both parties and results in committed follow-through on the solution. This does not suggest that analytical skills are not needed in negotiation, just that they are not paramount. They take up time and may get in the way of efforts that could be devoted to building an agreement.

Analytical skills may actually get
in the way of resolving conflicts.

Since good project and task force leaders must be skillful negotiators, each of the following nine techniques should be part of your repertoire:

1. *Be direct.* Act rather than react. Be a problem finder. Be clear about your interests and needs.

2. *Label behavior.* For clarity, make prefacing remarks during the negotiation. "What I'd like to do is propose . . ." and "May I make this suggestion . . ." reduces ambiguity about your intentions.

3. *Avoid argument.* Argument during the negotiation dilutes the process and gets people off the track of searching for and building upon agreements. Remember, arguments are emotional. They are seldom resolved with logic and facts.

4. *Be aware of the limitations of logic.* Rather than rely too heavily on logic and reason, try this attitude: "What seems reasonable to you is reasonable to me." Exchange statements play a pivotal role in this process. Sensitivity to others' perceptions is vital.

5. *Know what you want and ask for it.* If you don't know what you want, you can't ask for it. If you don't ask for it, you're not likely to get it. Nobody can read your mind, nor can you read anyone else's mind. Assertive expressions of needs, interests, and possible exchanges move the negotiations along.

6. *Repeat expectations firmly.* Persist in stating expectations, wants, and needs and in not letting the other person off too easily or making it easy for them to say no. By building on common ground, make it possible for the other person to say yes.

7. *Don't justify.* Too often, justification seems like rationalization and clutching at straws. Rather than justify defensively, make firm assertions backed by facts when appropriate.

8. *Avoid "irritants."* Words and phrases like: "Anyone could see that;" "it's always been done this way;" or "my generous offer" and the like push the other party into a corner where the only option is to fight or flee. Keep the discussion focused on the issues and not on personalities.

9. *Create alternative solutions.* Understand that both your own interests and those of others can probably be satisfied by more than one solution. Imagination is required both to understand and to use what you have that the other person wants or needs, and vice versa. Often this entails numerous "What if" statements. Inflate trial balloons and float them for possible agreement.

By effectively managing and negotiating conflicts, you will achieve positive outcomes from the inevitable differences that arise in moving your **GO-CARTS** forward. You can get the job done most effectively when you build agreements which vitalize participants. Conflict creates energy that is essential to managing projects and task forces from inception to implementation. Anticipating the sources of conflict and understanding the ebb and flow of conflicts in a project environment will increase your ability to harness this energy. Paradoxically, finding—or, if necessary creating—areas of agreement is an important starting place for negotiating differences.

SUMMARY: RULE NUMBER 8
VITALIZE PEOPLE BY BUILDING AGREEMENTS

1. Learning to manage conflicts rather than avoid them can help team leaders reach their goals. Conflict represents an emotional commitment to a project and when kept under control can lead team members to solve problems cooperatively.

2. Different sources of conflict generally arise over the life cycle of a project or task force. By knowing when and why these conflicts can occur, you can learn to channel team members' energies.

3. To resolve conflicts: create a common ground, enlarge areas of agreement, gather information, and focus on issues, *not* personalities.

4. In negotiating conflict, remember that both parties must come away satisfied, not just rationally but emotionally.

```
G               Develop People and Teams
 O                 Reinforce Commitment and Excitement
  C                    Inform Everyone
   A                      Vitalize by Building Agreements
    R                         E
     T                         R
      S
```

9

Rule Number Nine

EMPOWER YOURSELF AND OTHERS

It is powerlessness that corrupts. To truly empower others, you must give power away.

GO-CARTS can't get anywhere without power and the same is literally true for you. Finding mechanisms for enhancing your personal power and being able to correspondingly empower others is the challenge for winning projects, effective task forces, and high-performing work teams. Empowerment (the "E" in DRIVER) creates the energy necessary for sustained achievements.

Interestingly enough, everyone wants power. Few people feel they have enough of it. Haven't you heard these laments? "If I only had the authority necessary to get those people on track . . .". "If only I had the power to influence my superiors. . ." "What I need to get this done is more authority . . .". No matter what level of managers we have worked with, regardless of setting or function, all have felt that their situation would be better if only they had *more power*.

We have all been taught to associate power with authority and with one's location in the hierarchy of an organization—in other words, "position power." This is a restricted view of power. It assumes that power is a fixed-sum commodity and that there is only so much to go around. This viewpoint is limiting and contrary to what powerful project managers understand: that power is dynamic, and like electricity it is all around us, virtually infinite in its potential. Your challenge is to find ways to tap into this energy and to harness and channel its forces. Like putting money in the bank, power is a source of credit that expands with use and makes other people feel stronger and richer, too.

Literally, the word *power* means "to be able." Making something happen arises at least as much from personal competencies as it does from resources associated with one's position. Mike Badawy argues in his book *Developing Managerial Skills in Engineers and Scientists* that "of the two types of power, positional and personal, the project manager's authority is actually based on power which largely stems more from one's personal abilities and less from one's position."

Personal power is a set of skills and abilities possessed by an individual. It refers to ways we work with and respond to others in face-to-face situations. Most important, it does not come with an "office" but travels with each individual.

WHERE POWER COMES FROM

Power has been conceptualized as coming from at least one of six sources:

1. **Reward power,** based on our perception that another person has the ability to reward or grant resources that we desire
2. **Coercive power,** based on our perception that another person has the ability to punish or withhold valued resources from us
3. **Legitimate power,** based upon our internalized belief that another person, like the "boss", has the legitimate right to request certain types of actions and that we have a social obligation to comply with the request; often called "institutional power" or "formal authority"
4. **Referent power,** based on our desire to identify with another person and our belief that going along with the person's requests will facilitate a favorable interpersonal relationship and foster mutual respect

5. **Expert power,** based on our perception that another person has some special knowledge or information relevant to the task or problem at hand

6. **Relationship power,** based on our feeling that a caring work relationship exists between ourselves and another person.

The first three sources of power (reward, coercive, and legitimate) form the basis of position power. They are lodged in the position that the person holds. The last three (referent, expert, and relationship) form the sources of personal power. They reside in the personal characteristics of the position holder. There are limits to the amount of position power that you can use. For example, how many times can you fire someone? How often can you give someone a raise or promotion? And, more important, how often does a project or task force leader even have this kind of power? By contrast, there is virtually no limit to the amount of personal power that one person may possess in relation to another.

HOW POWER IS DISTRIBUTED

Researchers who have investigated why one branch, department, or unit of a company is more effective than another similar branch, department, or unit working under identical company policies, procedures, and organizational structures have identified power and its distribution as a key factor.

A consistent finding is that managers in the underachieving units hoard power. In the high-performing units, the managers share power. Consequently, people at every level in the high-performing units feel that they can, and should, be responsible for their unit's effectiveness. Contemporary management thought holds that it is powerlessness that corrupts and not vice versa. There is a rope all along the assembly line at the New United Motors Manufacturing, Inc. (NUMMI), plant, a joint venture between General Motors and Toyota. Any employee can pull that rope and shut down the assembly line in order to correct a manufacturing problem. Defects and waste have declined substantially since the rope was installed. As demonstrated at NUM-

MI, when people feel that they have power, they feel that they can make a difference, and productivity improves. Noah's teammates probably felt that if they didn't think something was right, they could take this directly up to the top!

Others studies of effective project managers and task force leaders have reported several significant relationships between performance and the use of various power bases. For example, the less team members perceive project managers or task force leaders as using position power and the more they perceive them using personal power, the greater are the levels of member involvement and openness of upward communication, and the higher is the productivity level of the team. Similar findings emerge from other studies involving such diverse occupations as sales personnel, college teachers, insurance underwriters, postal service carriers, and assembly-line workers.

Effective project leaders build and rely on personal sources of power.

GUIDELINES FOR THE EFFECTIVE USE OF POWER

People respond in one of three ways when you use power. They may demonstrate *commitment* to your request and enthusiastically engage in the desired behavior. They may *comply;* they go along with your request because they feel they have to, but they probably do not do anything beyond what is minimally required. Or they may *resist* by failing to follow through or by fighting back. Obviously, you need to understand how the various power bases can be used to generate commitment or, at least, willing compliance rather than resistance to your requests. And in doing this, you must also use your sources of power to empower others.

Building and Using Referent Power

You develop referent power when others on the project respect and admire you personally. This source of power is determined by the way you treat people. For example, showing consideration for their needs and feelings, dealing with each person fairly, and standing up for the group are ways to increase referent power. Face-to-face interaction with each individual on the team is essential.

Another way you create referent power is by setting an example. You should intentionally set an example of what you expect and want from others. In fact, you really can't ask anyone else to do something you would not be willing to do yourself without being hypercritical. When Daryl Leonard-Hartley, chief executive officer at Hyatt Hotels, wanted to underscore the importance of customer service, he donned a bellman's uniform and worked the lobby of the Chicago Hyatt. If quality, for example, is important, you need to emphasize quality in all you do, from the products you produce to the correspondence you send out. If quality is important, make it the first item on every meeting's agenda and the first question you ask when reviewing the project's progress with individuals on the team. Whenever Noah met with God, what do you think they talked about *first?* A major reason for Noah's commitment to the ark project was his trust (faith) in God.

Building and Using Relationship Power

Relationship power is developed by getting to know your people and by using the skill of listening (which we focused on with Rule Number 7). We can all relate to the fact that we will do more for a friend than for an acquaintance. As you get to know members of the project team or task force, and just as important, as they get to know you, you develop a sense of commitment toward each other.

The driving force behind developing these relationships has to be the project leader. If you risk letting people get to know you and take an interest in them, a sense of family begins to develop. And it is this sense of family that gets people committed and wanting to put forth their best efforts on the project. Harry Quadracci of Quad Graphics is a good example of a CEO who uses relationship power. By taking a genuine interest in his people, and by letting them get to know him (even his love of playing the saxophone), he builds relationships that yield commitment from employees that is above and beyond the call.

On a day-to-day basis, relationship power is also developed as we listen attentively to project team members. What are their concerns, their personal goals? What is happening in their lives? Not that you should necessarily try to solve their personal problems, but the empathy that comes from listening lets them know you care. And people generally go the extra mile for someone they know cares for them.

Building and Using Expert Power

You can't influence others just because you're the technical expert. Others must recognize that you are competent and perceive you to be a credible source of information and advice. Several factors help facilitate this process—for example, making sure that others are aware of your formal education, relevant work experience, and significant accomplishments. Also, you need to stay current and up to date. You cannot maintain an image of expertise unless you keep up with the latest developments in your field and remain professionally active.

Expert power can be undermined by relying too heavily on logic and rational reasoning as persuasion tactics. A barrage of one-way communications often leaves others feeling backed into a corner. Two-way communication, in which you first uncover the feelings and concerns of each person and then deal with these in making a persuasive argument, is more effective. If, for example, people on your task force are concerned about the possible unfavorable consequences of a policy, you should propose ways to avoid such consequences or to deal with them if they cannot be avoided.

Be tactful. You will generally receive a negative reaction from people if you flaunt your expertise and experience. It is counterproductive to try to convince others by belittling their arguments or making them feel stupid. These feelings can be created if you treat the objections, concerns, or suggestions of others as unimportant, trivial, or insignificant. Recognizing the contributions of others, respecting their self-worth, and incorporating, when possible, their ideas into action plans encourages their perception of your expertise (and your good sense).

And besides, you may not always be *the* expert. It may be that others on the project team or task force are the subject matter experts. Noah, for example, may not have been the expert on sails for the ark. By drawing upon the expertise of knowledgeable team members, Noah could ensure a better ark (project output) while also demonstrating his ability to know what "he does not know." You need to be sufficiently familiar with the work and competencies of others, understanding their language (jargon) and respecting their problems and viewpoints so you can coordinate and integrate their efforts and activities. In this way, you achieve expert power, even though, strictly speaking, you are not the expert.

Project leaders use their position power to help empower others.

Using Legitimate Power

Authority is exercised by making a legitimate request. You will encounter less resistance if you make it easy for others to go along with your request. One way to do this is to make "polite" requests. This is especially important for project personnel who are likely to be sensitive to status differences and authority relationships (for example, someone older than you or someone with multiple supervisors). Polite requests generally use the word *please*.

Another way to make it easy to go along is to explain the reasons behind a request. Others are more likely to go along with your requests when they see them as consistent with agreed-upon task objectives. Sometimes it is helpful to review the decision process you used to arrive at an action plan with the team. By taking them through the process step by step, they can see why the decision was made and why other alternatives were rejected.

Finally, it is helpful when project personnel understand that your requests are within the scope of your authority. Linking requests with official documentation such as written rules, policies, contract provisions, and schedules is one way to do this. Just like Noah, it may not be sufficient to say "Trust me." It helps when subordinates perceive that a higher authority is on your side.

Using Reward Power

The most common way of using reward power is to offer tangible benefits to people if they go along with your requests. However, the ideal conditions for using reward power effectively seldom exist. Many project managers lack control over attractive financial rewards. Project participants often have interdependent tasks that make it difficult to use individual incentives. Furthermore, objective indicators of performance are not available for many kinds of tasks, and people's behavior is often not easily observable.

There are other problems with relying too heavily on rewards as a source of influence. You may obtain compliance with rules and policies by the promise of rewards, but you are unlikely to obtain the person's heart or commitment. Gary Yukl in his book *Leadership in Organizations* points out these problems. As he notes, when people perform tasks in order to obtain a promised reward, they perceive their behavior as a means to an end. This may tempt them to take shortcuts and neglect less visible aspects of the task in order to complete the assignment and obtain the reward. Few internal incentives are generated to motivate the individual to put forth any extra effort beyond what is required or to demonstrate any particular initiative in carrying out the task. Subsequently, their relationship with you tends to become defined in purely economic terms. Special rewards come to be expected every time something new or unusual is required. Most managers run out of tangible goodies, especially as expectations escalate. In addition, using reward power can lead to resistance and resentment because people feel you are manipulating them by the contingent ("If you will do this, I will do that") nature of the relationship.

Consequently, rather than using rewards as explicit incentives, you need to recognize and reinforce desired behavior more subtly. Focusing on rewarding intrinsic needs like recognition, self-esteem, and future opportunities for growth and challenge.

The use of reward power should supplement and strengthen your referent power base. Give rewards in a way that expresses your personal appreciation for team member's efforts and accomplishments. Studies show that recipients of rewards come to like people who repeatedly provide rewards in an acceptable manner. Interpersonal relationships are more satisfying when they are viewed as an expression of mutual friendship and loyalty rather than an impersonal economic exchange.

Using Coercive Power

Effective project managers avoid using coercive power except when absolutely necessary because it is likely to create resentment and erode their personal power base. With coercion there is no chance of gaining commitment. Even willing compliance is difficult to achieve.

Coercion is most appropriate when it is used to stop behavior detrimental to the organization (e.g., theft, sabotage, violation of safety rules, or insubordination). Strategies of "positive discipline," rather than scaring people with threats or sample doses of punishment, are directed toward inducing subordinates to assume responsibility for helping resolve the discipline problem. Here are some guidelines for using positive discipline:

- Let people know about the rules and penalties for violations.
- Administer discipline consistently and promptly.
- Provide sufficient warning before resorting to punishment.
- Get the facts before using reprimands or punishments.
- Stay calm and avoid appearing hostile.
- Use appropriate punishments.
- Administer warnings and punishments in private.

WHAT PEOPLE WANT FROM THEIR LEADERS

It is apparent that among these various sources, the central determinant of power is in the "eye of the beholder"—what counts is what others (your subordinates, peers, and associates) perceive. The way you handle yourself, people's interactions with you, your managerial style, and the like influence their perception of your power, and hence the effect you can have on their behavior.

What exactly is it that others expect of you? What do people expect from their leaders? A series of studies by James Kouzes and Barry Posner, involving thousands of managers, identified four personal characteristics that people admire, look for, and expect most from those whom they are *willing* to follow. What do you think these characteristics are? Think about how you would measure up—in the eyes of your team or task force members.

The most frequently mentioned characteristic is **honesty.** People want a leader who is truthful with them and who can be trusted. People judge your honesty by observing your behavior. Do you do what you say you are going to do, or not?

Sam Walton, founder and chairman of Wal-Mart Stores— rated by *Forbes* as one of the richest people in the country—told his employees that if they achieved their profit objectives, he would put on a hula skirt and dance down Wall Street. They did. And he did! Being honest is, of course, a game involving risk. The leader must be the first one to ante up.

People want to feel that their leaders are honest, competent, forward-looking, and inspiring.

The second most desired characteristic in leaders is **competence.** Before they will follow a request, people must believe that this person knows what he or she is doing. This does not necessarily involve functional or technical abilities. The specific kind of competence people look for is affected by many factors, including position in the hierarchy and economic condition of the company. You must also be willing to demonstrate your ability to recognize the competence or expertise of others around you. In doing so, you demonstrate your level of trust in others— not unlike the kind of trust you want others to feel toward you.

The third most frequently mentioned characteristic is having a **forward-looking sense of direction.** This trait should be a natural for project managers and task force leaders. People who lead are expected to know where they are going and to be concerned about the future of the enterprise. Constituents want to have a feeling for the destination that the leader has in mind: Where are we going? What will it be like there? For example, when your project takes you to a foreign location, what do you do? Get a map. Read about the place. Look at pictures. Talk to others who have been there. Seek professional advice about the important sites, or customs, or regulations. Find out where (or what) to eat, where to stay, where to shop. Your clarity about the target and the project objectives are akin to "magnetic north." With a compass you can more easily guide the team forward and keep it on course.

Finally, people expect leaders to be **inspiring.** It is important that you be seen as enthusiastic, energetic, and positive about the project. Being inspiring is not necessarily being an evangelist but it is being willing to let others know what you care about. Max Dupree, former chairman of Herman Miller Furniture, would ask his senior executives: "What would make you weep?" You cannot cheer-manage—this isn't a word in our lexicon because cheering involves emotion and energy. Fundamentally, to be inspiring you need to be able genuinely to express your vision and values with others involved with the project or on the task force.

Nora Watson, a newspaper editor, offers this insight: "I think most of us are looking for a calling, not a job. Most of us have jobs that are too small for our spirit." Her statement is a reminder that you must help people find a greater sense of purpose and worth in their day-to-day life on the job. Because of the strength of their own convictions, effective project managers and task force leaders inspire the confidence necessary for others to perform at their best.

You must help people find a sense of purpose
and worth in their work, for in this feeling is
empowerment.

And so what do these four central leadership attributes add up to? What does it mean to be honest? To be competent? To be forward-looking and inspirational? These characteristics are the essence of **credibility.** When you are perceived as trustworthy, as knowing what you are talking about, as dynamic and sincere, and as having a sense of direction, others will see you as credible. And when you have credibility, people are likely to comply with your requests and even more likely to demonstrate a sense of commitment in their follow-through regardless of the power source you use. Both you and others will feel empowered! And empowerment is the energy that allows you to use the full power of your supercharged **GO-CARTS,** as well as the project team.

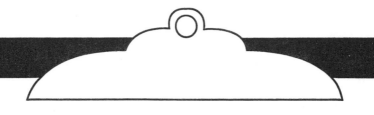

SUMMARY: RULE NUMBER 9
EMPOWER YOURSELF AND OTHERS

1. Most of the true power that project and task force leaders have comes from personal power, which derives from three sources: referent, expert, and relationship power.
2. Greater levels of project involvement and communication are found when leaders share power with team members.
3. People look for four personal characteristics in leaders: honesty, competency, a sense of direction, and inspiration.

<pre>
G   Develop People and Teams
 O   Reinforce Commitment and Excitement
  C   Inform Everyone
   A   Vitalize by Building Agreements
    R   Empower Yourself and Others
     T   R
      S
</pre>

10

Rule Number Ten

RISK
APPROACHING
PROBLEMS CREATIVELY

Those who want everything to be right the first time will never take the risk of innovating.

Risk taking completes the **DRIVER** acronym and is the final hurdle for successfully bringing your **GO-CARTS** to the checkered flag. Without opportunities to be innovative and daring, few races are won, even fewer projects are completed with quality on schedule and on budget, and few task force recommendations are implemented. Risk taking is the midwife to creativity.

There is no freeway to the future. To remain competitive in today's turbulent global marketplace every organization must be innovative. It is essential that organizations reward risk taking and encourage creativity. Project teams and task forces are often set up for the sole purpose of spurring process and product breakthroughs.

Creativity can be influenced. You can influence many of the factors identified as facilitating or hindering creative behavior. Innovative behavior in organizations is not simply a matter of selection, training, or good fortune.

We can look at the issue of creativity and innovation from the perspective of both the organization and the individuals on your team. However, it is useful to first explore what factors keep people from approaching problems creatively and how you might handle these.

BLOCKS TO CREATIVITY

Creative behavior is the expression of creative ability. One reason for the absence of creative behavior may be that people on your project team or task force feel inhibited from expressing their talents. Anxiety, fear of evaluation, defensiveness, and cultural inhibition are all blocks to the realization of creative potential. Managerial practices and organizational policies that foster such negative reactions hinder the expression of creative talent.

Organizations that stress the consequences of failure rather than the rewards for success tend to inhibit the expression of new ideas. Conversely, a climate that supports risk taking adopts the attitude of Thomas Edison: "I failed my way to success." Paul Cook, chairman at the highly innovative Raychem Corporation, puts it this way: "What gives me the greatest delight is the constant outpouring of new ideas."

Organizational instability can also inhibit creative expression. Unstable organizations are unpredictable to their members and breed insecurity and anxiety. But don't try to achieve stability through excessive formalization of rules, policies, relationships, and procedures. High levels of formalization interfere with interunit communications and discourage experimentation or the seeking of new alternatives or methods. Centralization restricts the free exchange of information and slows communications. These delays tend to dampen enthusiasm, increase response times, and heighten the probability that information is lost or distorted. A highly centralized organizational structure may inhibit the early stages of creativity and innovation.

Finally, leave time in your project for thinking and experimenting, for creative behavior. Take the attitude: "Don't just do something, sit there." The creative process takes time; how much time is not clear. When creativity is viewed as an unprogrammed activity, then the proposition "programmed work drives out unprogrammed work" comes into play. In such circumstances, the probability that project participants will make time for creative efforts is low. The highly innovative 3M Company guards against this by institutionalizing the bootlegging process. It expects all engineers and scientists to spend 15 percent of their time working on nonprogrammed activities. The IDEA program at Texas Instruments provides "on-the-spot" seed money to finance long-shot projects. The project does not need to obtain top management's approval.

Don't just do something, sit there.

FACILITATING CREATIVITY AND INNOVATION

Studies have identified reinforcement, goals, deadlines (like milestones), extended efforts, and freedom as facilitating creative efforts. By developing policies and practices that encourage individual creativity, you can develop and maintain higher levels of innovation. Let's explore these ideas in more detail.

Creative behavior, like any other type of behavior, is influenced by its outcome. When you ignore or punish risk taking, or when creative efforts are stifled, threatened, ridiculed, or stolen, creative energies are likely to be diminished. Even if creative talent has lain dormant, you can resurrect it through training and reinforcement. Often, you just have to let it out of the bottle. People have sometimes viewed creativity, like virtue, as its own reward. Certainly the intrinsic rewards in the satisfaction and feelings of accomplishment that accompany a creative insight or endeavor are powerful. Yet creative individuals, from scientists to toddlers, respond to extrinsic reinforcement as well.

Creative individuals need and respond to recognition, praise, and rewards. Consider, for example, that very few novels and even fewer (if any) scientific articles are published anonymously; composers copyright their music; artists sign their works. Inside the cover of Apple's Macintosh computer are the signatures of its entire design team.

Creative results are seldom anonymous.

Much of the world's great art, sculpture, and music has been produced on commission, as have many of the world's commercial innovations. Commissions not only provide monetary incentives, but they also facilitate innovation by setting guidelines as to expectations and deadlines for what is to be produced and when it is to be completed. Massive efforts in technological innovation grew from President Kennedy's goal of putting a man on the moon by 1970. Mozart finished one of the world's greatest operas by working through the night preceding its premiere. In many fields, time pressures can be outrageous *and* productive. It has been said that creative people in advertising work best while "under the gun." Deadlines and creativity are not necessarily in conflict.

Of course, the imposition of tight deadlines can be carried too far and can force acceptance of the first creative response. Evidence abounds that conscious efforts to avoid the immediate acceptance of "first" solutions can enhance creative effort. In several studies groups worked on problems until they arrived at a solution. They were then instructed to put that solution aside and to derive a second one. Invariably the second solutions were superior to the first, more conventional ones.

Individuals must be free to create. However, freedom and autonomy can be interpreted in vastly different ways. Certainly freedom from ridicule and fear is important, as are the opportunity and time to engage in preparation, incubation, reflection, and other elements of the creative process. Yet freedom and autonomy do not necessarily mean abandoning guidelines or constraints. Contrary to popular belief, creative individuals can live within budgets. One report analyzed 567 technical innovations in products or processes that occurred in 121 companies in five manufacturing industries. More than two-thirds cost less than $100,000; only 2 percent cost over $1 million. Individuals with complete freedom seldom get on track; among technical personnel, goals, budgets, and guidelines generally facilitate rather than hinder the creative process. The freedom in this case focuses on how to pursue an assignment as it relates to organizational goals.

Like any desired behavior, creativity must be identified, actively encouraged, recognized, rewarded, and used. Your challenge is to exercise sensitivity as to how best to provide reinforcement, goals and deadlines, extended effort, and a measure of freedom and autonomy in order to encourage creativity. Would the ark have ever been built on time or all the animals assembled two by two if Noah had wanted to approve every decision that was made? Clarity about the goal releases people's energies to pursue their tasks with enthusiasm.

**Deadlines and creativity are
not necessarily in conflict.**

Projects that have clear, operational objectives tend to provide goals and deadlines that aid creativity and innovation. The maxim "Necessity is the mother of invention" rings true. Project personnel who do not know what is necessary seldom find creative and innovative solutions to problems. Successful high-technology firms encourage their product development engineers to get out into the field. Unless this happens, there is a danger that the marketing identification of an opportunity will not get translated down to the product development engineers in a way that they can appreciate.

Similarly, when you support your project team and tolerate risk taking (and even failure), you can develop a climate in which high levels of creativity and innovation abound. Studies of managers who achieved extraordinary results in their organizations point out that people must be willing to challenge the process: "Those who want everything to be right the first time will never take the risk of innovating."

Creative behavior deals in uncertainty, which requires support and frequent communication at the interpersonal level. Open exchanges of information and exposure to new ideas fosters creative efforts. The Eleventh Commandment at the 3M Company is "Thou shalt not kill a new product idea." A great example of this is their Post-it™—notes, which everyone seems to find indispensable today. Initial reaction to the product was: "It's silly." Market surveys were negative. But the people at 3M continued to work with the idea for years until it began to gain acceptance—and a product was born that few of us can live without.

There is evidence as well that both flexibility and complexity in organizational design enhance the creative process. Flexibility permits the organization to adopt new and different ways of doing things. Complexity promotes specialization and autonomy. This means that project teams and task forces should be made up of individuals from diverse backgrounds and different specialties. This diversity stimulates creative productivity by providing people with opportunities to come up with new combinations and associations of ideas.

DEVELOPING BETTER IDEAS

Everyone has the potential to be creative! Keep this in mind when projects get bogged down and out of synch or when a timely, innovative solution is required to a difficult problem. You can either inhibit or facilitate creative expressions.

You should be on guard for the myriad "killer phrases" that crop up and tend to dampen creative energies. When pushed to their logical extremes they are illogical. Like any new seedling, an idea needs space, nourishment, and care until it can stand on its own. Killer phrases stomp on these ideas prematurely. So to the killer phrase statement, "But it's not in the budget!" you might respond "Of course not; we didn't have this idea when the budget was initially proposed," or "Do you mean to say that this organization won't support new ideas?" To the naysayers who exclaim, "We tried that before!" explain to them that "Now is different, in the following ways: . . .".

Being creative is within everyone's capability.

Better ideas can be developed through efforts to improve your ability and those of others in these four areas:

1. Problem sensitivity
2. Idea fluency

3. Originality

4. Flexibility

1. Problem sensitivity is the ability to recognize that a problem exists—to cut through misunderstanding, lack of facts, misconceptions, and other obscuring obstacles and perceive the real problem. In order to be a problem finder, not just a problem solver, requires you to develop early warning signs or identify potential red flags in the project life cycle that will warn you against the possibility of veering off course or going over a cliff. Additionally, you cannot assume constraints that don't exist. Equally important is that assumptions be frequently reevaluated as information changes and time goes by.

The most frequent reason for problem insensitivity is that we place imaginary restraints on problems. The famous Nine Dot puzzle in Figure 10.1 demonstrates this point. The problem requires you to draw four straight lines through all nine dots without retracing and without lifting your pencil from the paper. This can also be done with only three lines, two lines, and even one line! Try this puzzle for a moment or two.

What keeps many people from solving this problem imme-

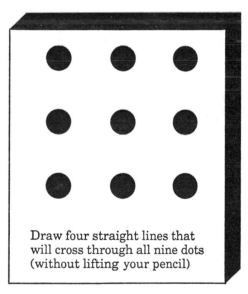

Draw four straight lines that
will cross through all nine dots
(without lifting your pencil)

Figure 10.1   An Example of Problem Insensitivity

diately is a nonexistent constraint or boundary—at least from the problem's viewpoint—that we place on the problem. Developing better ideas often requires you to test your assumptions, to go beyond your experiences, and possibly to bend the rules. In highly innovative organizations, people are apt to believe that "It's more fun to be a pirate than to join the Navy!"

2. Idea fluency is the ability to generate a large number of alternative solutions to a given problem in a given time. It is the law of large numbers, from statistical theory, applied to problem solving. In other words, the more ideas you have, the higher the probability that you will have good ideas. Robert Swerington, former chief executive officer at AMACO, was asked: "Why is your company so much more successful than your competitors at drilling wells which strike oil?" His reply "Because we drill more wells!"

In a classical brainstorming sense, you need to separate idea generation from idea evaluation. Premature evaluation stops the generation of new ideas. Furthermore, scholars of the innovation process have demonstrated quite persuasively that few ideas (concepts, processes, products) are immediate commercial successes. Night lighting for outdoor sports stadiums was several steps removed from the creation of iridescent lighting for ships at sea, and permeable face masks for coal miners were not the original intent of the inventors of disposable brassieres. Noah obviously asked for as many ideas as possible for determining the gender of porcupines besides just trying to pick them up.

3. Originality assumes many perspectives. In practical, day-to-day problem solving, complete newness or pure originality is usually not what you need. The originality you require is more likely to be that of finding new ways to vary existing conditions, new ways to adapt existing ideas to new conditions, or a new modification of something to fit an existing condition. Conditions that impede originality include stereotyping, saturation, and failing to use all of our sensory inputs.

Stereotyping is to some extent the difficulty people have in the nine-dot problem. We see a square even when one is not intended. Our imaginations are limited by our tendency to see what we expect to see. As you probably determined, the solution to the nine-dot problem is to go outside the *self-imposed* boundaries, as shown in Figure 10.2.

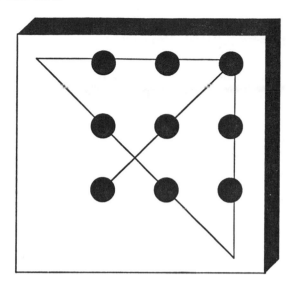

Figure 10.2 Going Outside the Boundaries Solves the Nine-Dot
Problem

Another factor that limits our ability to be original is called
saturation. The more familiar we are with a situation (person,
problem), the harder it is for us to see it in another context. Our
tendency is to see all problems alike or to see all problems
through a single filter (such as engineering, accounting, or public relations). For example, look at the list of numbers in Figure
10.3. See if you can determine the logic behind their particular
sequence.

Difficult? The vast majority of people approach this problem as a "numbers" or mathematical problem because that's the
form they found it in. There is no easy numbers solution (if one
is even possible!). But if you write out these numbers (for example, 11 becomes *eleven*), the solution becomes immediately apparent. Try it.

18, 11, 15, 14, 30, 12, 20

What is the logic behind this particular
sequencing of numbers?

Figure 10.3 An Example of Saturation

Too often we approach problems from a particular point of view, or stereotype, that limits our creative problem-solving ability. It also boxes people and departments in and limits their potential contributions—as in "Engineers can't talk with real customers," "Salespeople are more concerned about their customers than they are about this company," or "The accounting department always says no."

You also enrich your problem-solving ability when you use inputs from all of your senses (which are interconnected fairly directly). Visualization seems especially important. Friedrich Kekule, the famous chemist who discovered the structure of the benzene ring, did so in a dream after having devoted considerable conscious thought to its enigmatic structure. A delightful children's book is entitled *Put Your Mother on the Ceiling*. Children visualize this quite easily and naturally, but it is this same skill that enables the architect to imagine what a building will look like when completed (and how people will feel as they stroll through its lobby) or a computer programmer to write user-friendly software, or the personnel specialist to design stimulating recruitment strategies, or Noah to prepare an ark for The Great Flood.

4. Flexibility is the willingness to consider a wide variety of approaches to a problem (for example, the interests of all parties involved). Rather than zeroing in on a particular idea, technique, or viewpoint, you should start out by remembering that if one solution won't work, the problem can always be approached from another angle. Occasionally this requires a healthy skepticism about the obvious. As noted earlier, a group's first solution to a problem is generally less optimal than their second solution. You may have to push your project team or task force to generate that second solution or challenge them to go beyond the initial solution.

Flexibility is akin to idea fluency in asking you to view and understand a problem in different ways. What is the customer's viewpoint? How would this problem be perceived in the budget office? On the manufacturing floor? In the corporate boardroom? In the trade magazines?

Consider the case of the project engineer who was called to the building superintendent's office. The superintendent said that many complaints had been received about the elevators being too slow, and she wanted the engineer to solve this problem. What would you do?

A week passed, and the engineer announced he had a solution. The superintendent was delighted and expected to hear suggestions about increasing elevator speed, hydraulics, a new algorithm for sequencing the elevators during peak hours, or something similar. Instead the engineer proposed the installation of mirrors on each floor next to the elevators. If people were kept busy checking their appearance, he explained, they would have less time to notice the wait!

The boss had seen the problem as one of speeding up the elevators, but the engineer looked at the problem with flexibility. He chose to attack the impatience of the people waiting rather than the speed of the elevators. By failing to look at problems from different (multiple) perspectives, you often limit your creative potential.

Without rewarding risk taking and encouraging creativity it is difficult to imagine how Noah would have ever succeeded in building, launching, and navigating the ark. Bringing your **GO-CARTS** to the finish line first always requires some amount of ingenuity. The most stimulating and rewarding projects are somewhat like riding a roller coaster, never really knowing for sure where the dips, twists, and turns are but enjoying the challenge and being confident in your ability to stay on the ride to the end. Like the turtle, the most successful project managers and task force leaders realize that they make significant progress only when they stick their neck out.

To make significant progress
you have to stick your neck out.

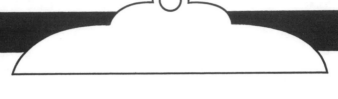

SUMMARY: RULE NUMBER 10
RISK APPROACHING PROBLEMS CREATIVELY

1. Contrary to what many people believe, creativity can be taught to people.
2. Before individuals can let themselves be creative, your job is to eliminate potential blocks to risk taking.
3. Goals and deadlines actually help to foster creativity.
4. Four strategies to encourage creativity are increased problem sensitivity, idea fluency, originality, and greater flexibility.

```
G          Develop People and Teams
 O            Reinforce Commitment and Excitement
  C              Inform Everyone
   A               Vitalize by Building Agreements
    R                Empower Yourself and Others
     T                 Risk Approaching Problems Creatively
      S
```

DRIVING
TO THE CHECKERED
FLAG

So there you have it—ten rules for managing your project team or task force to success. Adhering to the first four rules will enable you to develop a sound plan. A plan that is both strong yet flexible enough to handle the unexpected, but inevitable, problems. It will be a plan that your team members can commit themselves to. Your **GO-CARTS** will be capable of carrying you the distance, to the checkered flag.

The last six rules are designed to help you manage the project plan from beginning to end. They will help you anticipate problems before they become severe enough to knock you out of the race. Unexpected pit stops will be minimized and handled more efficiently by our team. Opportunities to move ahead will be recognized and seized because you will be navigating the course as a **DRIVER** who is well prepared and highly motivated to bring home the checkered flag.

So the key to going fast later is to go slow early. Take the time to build solid **GO-CARTS.** For each of your projects and task forces, remember to determine the

Goals for the project
Objectives for the project
Checkpoints to monitor progress
Activities to be completed
Relationships among the activities
Time estimates for the activities
Schedule for the project

Develop and strengthen your abilities as a **DRIVER** so that project and task force implementation goes smoothly. This is facilitated when you

Develop people individually and as a team
Reinforce people's commitment and excitement
Inform everyone connected with the project
Vitalize people by building agreements
Empower yourself and others
Risk approaching problems creatively

These are the ten rules followed by successful project team and task force leaders. Now that you know them and can understand how to apply these rules, *the only thing left for you to do is to begin using them.*

REFERENCE NOTES

THE CHALLENGE OF MANAGING PROJECT TEAMS AND TASK FORCES

PHILIP B. CROSBY, *Let's Talk Quality*. New York: McGraw-Hill, 1989.

THOMAS J. PETERS, *Thriving on Chaos*. New York: Alfred A. Knopf, 1987.

RULE NUMBER ONE

KENNETH BLANCHARD AND SPENCER JOHNSON, *The One Minute Manager*. New York: William A. Morrow, 1982.

JOAN KNUTSON, *How to Be a Successful Project Manager*. New York: American Management Association Extension Institute, 1980.

THOMAS J. PETERS AND ROBERT H. WATERMAN, JR., *In Search of Excellence*. New York: Harper & Row, 1982.

RULE NUMBER TWO

STEVEN KERR, "On the Folly of Rewarding A, While Hoping for B," *Academy of Management Journal*, 18 (1975):769–783.

ROBERT KREITNER, *Management*. Boston: Houghton-Mifflin, 1983.

LEONARD R. SAYLES, *Leadership: Managing in Real Organizations*, 2nd ed. New York: McGraw-Hill, 1989.

RULE NUMBER THREE

KENNETH BLANCHARD AND ROBERT LORBER, *Putting the One Minute Manager to Work*. New York: William A. Morrow, 1984.

LYNN STUCKENBRUCK, *The Implementation of Project Management: The Professional's Handbook*. Reading, MA: Addison-Wesley, 1981.

RULE NUMBER FOUR

RALPH L. KLEIN, *The Secrets of Successful Project Management*. New York: John Wiley, 1986.

JEROME D. WEIST AND FERDINAND K. LEVY, *A Management Guide to PERT/CPM*. Englewood Cliffs, NJ: Prentice Hall, 1977.

MAURICE ZELDMAN, *Keeping Technical Projects on Target*. New York: AMACOM, 1978.

RULE NUMBER FIVE

KENNETH H. BLANCHARD, DONALD CAREW, AND EUNICE PARISI-CAREW, *The One-Minute Manager Builds High Performing Teams*. Escondido, CA: Blanchard Training and Development, 1990.

ROSABETH MOSS KANTER, *The Change Masters*. New York: Simon & Schuster, 1983.

GEORGE E. MANNERS, JR., JOSEPH A. STEGER, AND THOMAS W. ZIMMERER, "Motivating Your R & D Staff," *Research Management*, 26, 5. (1983):12–16.

DEAN TJOSVOLD, *Team Organization*. New York: John Wiley, 1991.

RULE NUMBER SIX

TRACY KIDDER, *The Soul of a New Machine*. Boston: Little, Brown, 1982.

JAMES M. KOUZES AND BARRY Z. POSNER, *The Leadership Challenge: How to Get Extraordinary Things Done in Organizations*. San Francisco: Jossey-Bass, 1987.

GARY N. POWELL AND BARRY Z. POSNER, "Excitement and Commitment: Keys to Project Success," *Project Management Journal*, 15, 4 (1984):39–46.

RULE NUMBER SEVEN

ROBERT E. ALBERTI AND MICHAEL L. EMMONS, *Stand Up, Speak Out, Talk Back!* New York: Pocket Books, 1975.

CARL R. ROGERS AND RICHARD E. FARSON, "Active Listening," in D. A. Kolb, I. M. Rubin, and J. M. McIntyre (Eds.), *Organizational Psychology: Readings on Human Behavior in Organizations.* Englewood Cliffs, NJ: Prentice Hall, 1984.

PATRICK L. TOWNSEND (with Joan E. Gebherdt), *Commit to Quality.* New York: John Wiley, 1986.

RULE NUMBER EIGHT

CLIFFORD F. BOLSTER, "Negotiating: A Critical Skill for Technical Managers," *Research Management,* 27, 6 (1984):18–20.

ROGER FISHER AND WILLIAM URY, *Getting to Yes.* New York: Penguin Books, 1981.

CRAIG R. HICKMAN, *Mind of a Manager, Soul of a Leader.* New York: John Wiley & Sons, 1990.

BARRY Z. POSNER, "What's All the Fighting About in Project Management?" *IEEE Transactions in Engineering Management,* 33(4) (1986):207–211.

HANS J. THAMHAIN AND DAVID L. WILEMON, "Leadership, Conflict, and Program Management Effectiveness," *Sloan Management Review* 19, no. 1 (1977):69–89.

RULE NUMBER NINE

RUSSELL D. ARCHIBALD, *Managing High Technology Programs and Projects.* New York: John Wiley, 1976.

MICHAEL K. BADAWY, *Developing Managerial Skills in Engineers and Scientists.* New York: Van Nostrand Reinhold, 1982.

JAMES M. KOUZES AND BARRY Z. POSNER, "The Credibility Factor: What People Expect from Their Leaders," *Management Review,* 79(1) (1990):29–33.

GARY A. YUKL, *Leadership in Organizations,* 2nd ed. Englewood Cliffs, NJ: Prentice Hall, 1989.

RULE NUMBER TEN

JAMES ADAMS, *Conceptual Blockbusting*. Stanford, CA: Stanford Alumni Association, 1974.

JAN CARLSON, *Moments of Truth*. New York: Harper & Row, 1987.

ALBERT SHAPERO, *Managing Professional People: Understanding Creative Performance*. New York: Free Press, 1985.

ACKNOWLEDGMENTS

It is with pleasure that we acknowledge the insights, information, and encouragement afforded us by others. First, to the thousands of people who have attended our Project Management Cross-Functional Teams and Task Force Management seminars; as we wrote this book, we had you in mind.

A special thanks to the following colleagues who reviewed the entire manuscript and provided additional examples, informative suggestions, and good cheer:

Cheryl Breetwor
President
ShareData, Inc.
Sunnyvale, California

Stephen Carter
President
Carter, Goble Associates,
Inc.
Columbia, South
Carolina

Kim Detiveaux
Management Development
Representative
Pacific Gas & Electric
Company
San Francisco, California

John Donnelly
Information Systems
Manager
Siemens Medical Systems
Iselin, New Jersey

John Harrison
Director of Planning and
Analysis
Baskin-Robbins, Inc.
Glendale, California

Randy Lamkin
Management
Development Director
Richland Memorial
Hospital
Columbia, South
Carolina

Ronald Luman
  Missile Analysis
    Supervisor
  Applied Physics
    Laboratory
  Johns Hopkins University
  Laurel, Maryland

Robert Phillips
  President
  Robert H. Phillips Group
  Emeryville, California

Victor Robinson
  Engineering Manager
  Mid-West Conveyor
    Company
  Kansas City, Kansas

Jeff Samet
  Vice President
  Consulting Group
  W. C. Pinkard and
    Company, Inc.
  Baltimore, Maryland

George W. Summerson, Jr.
  Division Manager
  Hoechst-Roussel
    Pharmaceutical, Inc.
  Columbia, South
    Carolina

Mark Tager
  President
  Great Performance, Inc.
  Chicago, Illinois

Charles White
  Executive Director
  Sigma Phi Epsilon
    Fraternity Foundation
  Richmond, Virginia

Steve Willard
  President
  Steve Willard and
    Associates
  Portland, Oregon

Linda Wilshusen
  Executive Director
  Transportation
    Commission
  Santa Cruz County
  Santa Cruz, California

We also want to thank Ken Blanchard, Pat Zigarmi, and Drea Zigarmi (all of Blanchard Training and Development), Gary Powell (University of Connecticut), Jim Kouzes (The Tom Peters Group), and Brian Robinson (Santa Clara University). We have learned a great deal from them in joint research efforts and management development seminars. They are sure to recognize their handiwork in this material. Of course, all responsibility for any shortcomings remain ours.

A very special and grateful note of appreciation to our wives, Jackie Schmidt-Posner and Ruth Anne Randolph. Jackie and Ruth Anne read the entire manuscript and offered both substantive and editorial suggestions. Liz Currie (Santa Clara University) did a masterful job editing the manuscript and Elizabeth Caravelli (Santa Clara University) typed and retyped the manuscript with remarkable efficiency and care. Thank you.

Finally, this project was tough, challenging, and fun. We both spent considerable effort to define and clarify our goals and objectives, to keep on schedule, to recognize each other's strengths and tensions, to find common ground, to be honest with each other, and to provide support, encouragement, and critical reflections. We determined the order of authors by a flip of the coin. We think we got the job done!

INDEX